Spanish for Geniuses:
Advanced classes to get you speaking with fluency and confidence

By Andromeda Jones

Copyright © 2016 by Andromeda Jones

All rights reserved. No part of this publication may be reproduced, distributed, or transmitted in any form or by any means, including photocopying, recording, or other electronic or mechanical methods, without the prior written permission of the publisher, except in the case of brief quotations embodied in critical reviews and certain other noncommercial uses permitted by copyright law. For permission requests, write to the publisher, addressed "Attention: Permissions Coordinator," at the address below.

Printed in the United Kingdom

www.bilinguanation.com

Publisher's Cataloging-in-Publication data

Jones, Andromeda.

Spanish for Geniuses/ Andromeda Jones.

1. Spanish language learning. 2. Spanish grammar and vocabulary

Contents

Introduction..6

1. Nouns and articles..10
2. Adjectives...18
   Comparatives and superlatives..21
   Adjectives advanced..24
3. Possessives...26
4. Pronouns..29
   Interrogative pronouns...29
   Object pronouns...31
   Direct and indirect object pronouns..32
   Prepositional pronouns..34
   Relative pronouns...35
5. The present tense..40
6. Present tense questions and adverbs of frequency..50
7. Gustar and back to front verbs..53
8. Infinitives...55
   Infinitives advanced...57
9. Obligation, ability and deduction..58
   Obligation: Must, have to, should...58
   Ability: Poder, podria..60
   Making deductions: Must be, should be...62
   Possibility: May and might...63
10. Giving orders: The imperative tense..65
11. The future..69
12. The conditional tense...74
13. The past..77

The preterite 77

The imperfect 79

14. Between the past and present: The perfect tense 87

The past perfect – there was 90

16. Reflexives 95

17. The subjunctive in present 102

18. The past subjunctive and if clauses 115

    Even though and Even if 120

Mixed conditionals 122

Ojalá – wish or hope 123

19. The pluperfect subjunctive 125

20. Making suppositions 127

21. Ser versus Estar 131

22. All the forms of haber 140

23. The passive and its alternatives 142

24. Become and other verbs that express change 145

25. Whatever, no matter and ever 150

Not even and even 152

26. Reported speech 153

27. Adverbs 155

Still, already, yet, anymore 155

Just 156

General Adverbs 157

28. Some, any and nothing 159

    Tampoco 164

29. How much, how many and other quantities 165

Todo/a and todos/as – All, everything and everybody 168

30. Too, enough, so much, so many, so 170

31. Prepositions...173

How do you say?..179

32. Speaking about time..180

33. The weather..188

34. Measuring length and depth...190

35. Measuring distance and directions...191

36. Receiving services...193

37. Chatting with friends..199

38. Appearance and personality...212

39. Talking about feelings and physical states...217

40. Body positions and movements...227

41. Forming an argument...230

42. Dealing with situations...239

43. Work and business..248

44. Education and ability..250

45. Verb families...252

46. What's the verb?.. 257

47. Collocations..260

48. Writing..262

Additional information..264

Introduction

You picked this book because you're learning Spanish. Not just a few holiday phrases – a 'buenos días' or 'dame un café' – no you want to speak with fluency in a wide variety of conversations or even master the language if you can.

But why in a world where so many speak English do we embark on such a journey nowadays?

Well everyone has their reasons but most agree on one thing – speaking a foreign language, even at the most basic level, is exciting.

You know the scene. You're at a restaurant in a foreign country and the waitress appears. You open your mouth and in another language a few halting words work their way out. You wonder if anything you've said has made sense. But yes, incredibly she has understood and replies. You understand her also or at least enough to muddle through and complete your order.

Probably no one else present will have understood what you just accomplished. But you know and the work it took to get there and now you may find yourself wondering; how far could you take this? With a few more months of study could you get to a good conversational level? With a few more years could you pass for fluent?

All of this is possible – but how do you get there?

I chose the title Spanish for Geniuses not because only a genius can learn a language but because there are certain genius ways to learn it quicker and more proficiently than the traditional study route. Let's start with the grammar.

The grammar
Yes, learning grammar is hard work and no, you can't do it in a month as some books claim but there are hacks to help you learn it quicker and thereafter make fewer mistakes.

Hack one is to recognise that though Spanish is a foreign language it is not an alien one. It is actually very similar to English both in verb tenses and expression.

Don't believe me? Take a look at these sayings:

'Matar dos pajaros con un tiro' – To kill two birds with one stone.

'Llevarse como el perro y el gato' – To fight like cat and dog.

'Coger el toro por los cuernos' – To take the bull by its horns.

'Es pan comida' – It's a piece of cake.

'Dicho y hecho' – All said and done.

In my decade of learning and speaking Spanish I have found around 80% of sentence structure and tenses to be the same or similar to English. Part I of Spanish for Geniuses teaches verb tenses, noun, adjective, adverb, preposition and pronoun rules with detailed explanations about how they relate to English. But what about the other 20%?

The differences
Well, this is where students will slip up because the sentence structure or tense is different. Differences can be discouraging. I am an English teacher and I have had many a Spanish student trying to learn our language declare they'll never speak proficiently because of all the differences.

What students often fail to recognise is that differences are your friend. If you take 80% of the languages to be the same or similar then you only have to learn the 20% to eliminate your mistakes.

Sure it's going to take time and practice but it is achievable and to help you the book highlights all Spanish/English differences in their own box outs with clear explanations to help you speak correctly

The words
You've done learning the grammar and you've memorised the differences. Now you travel to a Spanish speaking country expecting to make at least passable conversation but when you open your mouth nothing comes out. Why is this?

Well it's because you're missing a vital component in your language armoury. You may know which words to use and in what tense but you lack the knowledge of *how* to say it.

When I first started learning a guy I knew, who was an English/Spanish bilingual, advised me to learn phrases rather than words. Many miscommunications and awkward moments later, I finally got what he meant. Vocabulary is important, of course, but you cannot translate word for word the sentences you're used to saying in English.

The equivalent would be a Spanish speaker walking into a café in London and saying 'give me a coffee.' The bar tender would understand what he *meant* but there would be a raised eyebrow or two as the proper (and polite) way to say this is 'can I have a coffee.'

The same is true of Spanish. Their way of speaking is often not quite the same as ours and so a broad knowledge of phrases is essential.

The second half of Spanish for Geniuses opens the door onto the way Spanish speakers really speak with phrases and tip bits to make thousands of conversations from chatting with friends, organising, negotiating, receiving a service or solving an emergency. You need it? You'll find it there.

About this book

This book is written for English speakers who wish to learn Spanish to a high level. For this reason it talks a lot about the way we use our native language as I discovered when teaching English that understanding how our own grammar works is the key to understanding the grammar of other foreign languages.

As I live in Spain the emphasis is on Castilian Spanish but it can be applied to South American also as, with the exception of Argentina and Uruguay, there are only a few differences in vocabulary and pronunciation.

About the author

I am a British English teacher teaching in Spain. Ten years ago I started out like you – learning Spanish though my own interest. Somewhere along the way I got ambitious and started noting and categorising the phrases people used around me to create a resource that went way beyond traditional Spanish language books.

I published because I figured that there were others out there like me who could use them. Those being the *afictionados* – the people who wanted to do more than order a meal –the people who want to know everything – or at least as much as the could.

This is why I wrote Spanish for Geniuses. For Geniuses like you.

1. Nouns and articles

Gender

A good place to start are nouns. Spanish nouns are either masculine or feminine. Most of the time it is easy to tell them apart as masculine nouns end in 'o' and feminine 'a' such as 'el bolígrafo' or 'la manzana'.

Nouns with the following endings are masculine:

-aje: El paisaje (the landscape), El equipaje (the equiment), El reciclaje (the recycling).

- án: el desván – (the attic).

- or: el amor (love), el valor (courage). Exceptions are la flor (flower), la coliflor (cauliflower) la labor (task).

- ambre: el alambre (the wire), el hambre (hunger)

In addition, all nouns ending in a vowel with an accent are masculine. This includes El sofá, el café, and el champú.

Nouns with the following endings are feminine:

-dad (This is 'ity' in English): La ciudad (the city), La calidad (quality).

-ión: La dirección (the address), La estación (the station), la información (the information).

-tad: La virtud (virtue), la dificultad (the difficulty), La libertad (liberty).

-umbre: La certidumbre (the certainty), la muchedumbre (the crowd).

-ie: La serie (the series), la especie (the species).

-isis: La crisis (the crisis), la dosis (the dose).

The irregulars
There is a small list of nouns that do the exact opposite.

Feminine nouns ending in 'o'
'La foto' (the photo), 'la moto' (the motorbike), 'la mano' (the hand), 'la radio' (the radio), 'la disco.'

Masculine nouns ending in 'a'

'El día' (the day), 'el mapa' (the map), 'el yoga', 'el planeta' (the planet), 'el tranvía,' (the tram) 'el guía' (the guide).

In addition, many nouns ending in 'ma' are also masculine. These include: 'El clima' (the climate), 'el problema' (the problem), 'el sistema' (the system), 'el programa' (the program), 'el tema' (the subject), 'el drama' (the drama), 'el síntoma' (the symptom), 'el pijama' (pyjamas), 'el fantasma' (the ghost).

But there are a few 'ma' nouns that remain feminine. For example, 'la cama' (the bed), 'la pluma' (the feather) and 'la forma' (the shape).

Other masculine nouns
Compound nouns
Compound nouns are two nouns joined together to form a new meaning. They are also masculine even if they end in an 'a'. For example:
'El parabrisas' (windscreen), 'el paraguas' (umbrella), 'el sacacorchos' (the corkscrew), 'el lavaplatos' (the dishwasher), 'el abrelatas' (the can-opener).

Languages
The names of languages are also masculine. For example:
'El inglés' (English), 'el alemán' (German), 'el italiano' (Italian).

Professions
Many professions end in an 'o' for male workers and an 'a' for female. For example:

La profesora/el profesor	The teacher
La médica/el medico	The doctor
La abogada/el abogado	The lawyer

In some professions, however, the noun remains the same and only the article changes.

La/el cantante	The singer
La/el periodista	The journalist
La/el modelo	The model

People

Titles for people also end in 'o' for masculine and 'a' for feminine. For example:

Amiga y amigo – female friend and male friend.

Abuela y abuelo – grandmother and grandfather.

Hermana y hermano – sister and brother.

Hija e hijo – daughter and son.

Niña y niño – girl and boy.

Novia y novio – girlfriend and boyfriend.

To refer to these people in plural, use the masculine form and attach an 's'. If the group is all female, however, use the feminine form plus 's'.

For example:

'Mis hermanos viven en Madrid' – My siblings live in Madrid.

Plural rules

To make nouns plural you add 's' to a vowel or 'es' to a consantant. However there are some variations:

Words ending in 'z' change to 'ces' – for example, 'vez' (time) and 'veces' (times).

Words ending in a stressed –án, -én, -ín, -ón lose their accent when plural.

Words ending in a stressed –í or –ú should add 'es' – for example, 'los champúes' (the shampoo).

Definite article: The / el, la, los, las

The definite article is 'the' in English. It identifies the one out of a group of nouns that you are speaking about. For example, 'give me the pen' means not just any pen but the one that I want.

Spanish definite articles operate in much the same way as English but they change depending on the gender of the noun.

Masculine nouns are preceded by 'el' – such as 'el árbol' (the tree) and feminine nouns are preceded by 'la' such as – 'la mesa' (the table).

When this is not true

If the noun starts with a strong 'a' sound the article is 'el'. This happens even if the noun is feminine. For example, 'agua' (water) is feminine, but, when placed with the definite article it is 'el agua.'

This happens because if you were to say 'la agua' then your tongue would trip over itself while trying to pronounce two separate 'a' sounds so close together. We do the same thing in English by using 'an' with nouns that start with vowels. Imagine saying 'a apple,' not so easy, eh?

More examples of feminine nouns beginning with 'el':

'el águila' (the eagle), 'el aula' (the classroom), 'el alma' (the soul), 'el arma' (the weapon), 'el hacha' (the axe), 'el hambre' (the hunger).

Plurals

Plural nouns are preceded by 'los' if they are masculine – for example, 'los coches' and 'las' for feminine, 'las plantas'.

Del and al

If your sentence has de + el put them together to form del.

If it has a + el put them together to form al.

For example: 'Vamos al parque' – we are going to the park and 'la ventana del edificio' – the window of the building/the building's window.

[Spanish/ English Difference] When the article is and is not used

It is not used:

When referring to 'The Internet.' It is 'me gusta Internet' – I like Internet, not *the* Internet.

When referring to monarchs or cities. For example:

'Felipe, Rey de España' or 'Londres, capital de Reino Unido.'

When the article is used

El, la, los and las are used when we would use 'the' in English, but:

- They are also used for abstract concepts such as 'love', 'quality', 'health', 'nature' – 'el amor', 'la calidad', 'la salud', 'la naturaleza,' respectively. We don't do this in English –possibly because most of the time these refer to things you can't see. But just because you can't see them does not mean they are not objects, which is why Spanish speakers do still use the article.

- 'El' and 'los' are also used for days of the week. In English we would use the preposition 'on.'

For example:

'El sábado juego un partido de fútbol' – on Saturday I'll play a football match.

If this event occurs on multiple Saturdays then use the article 'los.'

For example:

'Los domingos paso tiempo con mi familia' – on Sundays I spend time with my family.

Indefinite article: A, an / un, una, unos, unas/algunos, algunas

The indefinite article is 'a' or 'an' in English and is used to talk about any one of a group. For example, 'give me a pen,' now you don't want one in particular (the pen), any pen will do.

'Un' precedes masculine nouns such as 'un bolígrafo', 'un libro' (a book) while 'una' precedes feminine nouns for example, 'una mesa', 'una bolsa' (a bag).

> [Spanish/English difference] **When to use the indefinite article**
>
> 'Un' and 'una' can be translated as 'a' in English but there are a couple of important differences:
>
> You don't use the indefinite article:
>
> **With professions:** For example, 'soy maestra' (I am **a** teacher) or 'Es ingeniero' (He is **an** engineer).
>
> **After 'sin' ('without') or 'qué' ('what' or 'how'):**
>
> For example:
>
> 'Sale sin chaqueta' – 'He goes out without a jacket'
>
> 'Qué sorpresa la fiesta' – 'What a surprise the party was.'
>
> **When speaking about something that is not concrete:** This is a little tricky – in English we use 'a' or 'an' for things that are definitely real such as 'there is a cat in the room'. However, we also use it for things that might not be real, such as 'is there a queue at the bank right now?' or 'do you have a pen?'
>
> In Spanish this would be '¿hay cola en el banco ahora mismo? and '¿tienes coche?
>
> The reason why the 'un' or 'una' is omitted is that you can only use it to refer to something that you are sure exists or used to exist. You don't know whether your friend has a pen or that there is a queue at the bank. For this reason the indefinite article is hardly ever used in questions or negatives.

Plurals

If the items you want are plural then you use 'unos' for masculine and 'unas' for feminine. This can be translated as 'some' in English.

For example:

'Pásame unos libros' – pass me some books.

As an alternative to 'unos/unas' you can also use 'algunos/algunas'. Most of the time the two can be used interchangeably, however there are a few subtil difereces.

Unos / unas versus algunos / algunas

Unos: When making an approximation you use 'unos' and not 'algunos'. For example:

'Hay unas cincuenta sillas en la sala de reuniones' – there are some fifity chairs in the meeting room.

Algunos: In the case of 'some of', 'algunos de' is far more used that 'unos de'. For example:

'Hay algunos de mis papeles en el estante' – there are some of my papers on the shelf.

'Algunas de las montañas mas altas existen en Asia' – some of the tallest mountains exist in Asia.

Also: if the sentence contrasts with 'none' or 'no one' then algunos/as is more common. For example:

'Algunas personas les gusta la morcilla' – some people like blood sausage (as opposed to no one).

'Algunos empleados trabajan durante el fin de semana' – some employees work at the weekend.

Diminutives and augmentatives

Diminutives

In English we put a 'y' at the end of nouns to emphasise their smallness, such as the words 'doggy' or 'blanky.' Spanish does the same thing. To create a diminutive, drop the '-o' or '-a' from the noun and add '-ito' or '-ita'. Add '-cito' or '-cita' to words not ending in 'o' or 'a'. For example:

'Perrito' – (doggy).

'Bolsito' – (little bag).

'Mesita' – (little table).

'Cochecito' – (little car).

Augmentatives

Spanish nouns and adjectives can also be changed to imply largeness (and also often 'undesirable'). There are many ways to do this, but, the two most popular endings are –ón/-ona and -azo/-aza. For example:

'Copión' – Big cheat in exams.

'Comilón' – Big eater.

'Exitazo' – Great success.

'Perrazo' – Big, mean dog.

'Portazo' – To slam the door.

2. Adjectives

Adjectives in Spanish usually (but not always) go after the noun and match its gender by changing their ending to 'o' or 'a,' for example, 'la niña alta', or 'el coche blanco.'

It is worth noting, that only the colours 'negro' (black), 'blanco' (white), rojo (red) and 'amarillo' (yellow) change depending on the gender of the noun as the others cannot change their endings.

More adjectives that don't change their endings
Here is a selection of a few more adjectives that don't change:
Difícil/fácil – difficult/easy.
Feliz/triste – happy/unhappy (the synonym 'contento,' however, does change gender).
Fuerte – strong.
Natural – natural.
Optimista/pesimista – optimistic/pessimistic.

Plurals
Unlike English, if the noun is plural then the adjective is plural –such as, 'las casas blancas' or 'los perros negros.' This is usually easy to learn as it is perfectly logical.

Nationalities are also, without exception, plural –for example, 'los ingleses' (the English) or 'los alemanes'- (the Germans). Note that nationalities are not capitalised.

Negatives
Spanish speakers hardly ever use prefixes to make adjectives negative (such as 'uninteresting'). Instead they use:
'No' – 'no es común' (it isn't common or it is uncommon).

'Sin' – 'es un problema sin solucionar' (it is an unsolvable problema).

'Poco' – this does not mean in this case 'little' or 'few' but rather 'not much' or 'not very,' for example:

'El hombre es poco inteligente' – the man is not very intelligent.

Styles and materials

This is relatively easy .Simply add 'de' and the noun. For example:

'La mesa es de madera' – the table is wooden (or literally 'The table is of wood').

This way of speaking means that you can quickly make complicated descriptions without learning a long list of adjectives. Check out these material words:

De flores – flowery.
De lunares – spotted.
De seda – silky.
De piel – leather.
De lana – woollen.

[Common mistakes] Adjective order

Most of the time adjectives go after the noun but this is not <u>always</u> the case. Compared to English, Spanish actually has very few adjectives, so Spanish speakers change their position to create a second meaning.

Generally speaking an adjective placed after the noun classifies the noun in terms of colour, size, material or speed and so on, while an adjective before the noun adds emotion.

It is important to note, however, that many before-noun adjectives are not found in everyday speech and are usually only used in poetry and literature. I shall mark when this occurs below.

For example: 'La noche oscura' means 'the dark night' and 'la oscura noche' means 'The creepy night' (poetic term).

Here are some more examples:

Adjectives before the noun	Adjectives after the noun
Mi viejo amigo –My old friend	Mi amigo Viejo –My physically old friend.
El triste hombre *-The wretched man	El hombre triste –The sad mad.
La antigua silla –The old-fashioned chair.	La silla antigua –The old chair.
El nuevo libro –Brand new book	El libro nuevo –Newly issued book.
La pobre mujer –The pitiful woman.	La mujer pobre –The poor (no money) woman.
Mis propios zapatos –My own shoes.	Mis zapatos propios –My appropriate shoes.
Un solo hombre –Only one man.	Un hombre solo – A lonely man.
Un triste viaje * - A dreadful trip	Un viaje triste – A sad trip.
La única estudiante –The only student.	La estudiante única –The unique student.
La gran empresa –The great company.	La empresa grande –The big company

*Poetic term.

Adjectives that must go before the noun

There are some adjectives that always go before the noun. These are 'mejor' (better), 'peor' (worse), primero (first), 'segundo' (second), 'tercero' (third) and so on.

Buen, mal, gran

When bueno, malo, and grande go before a masculine noun they drop the last letter.
For example:
'El buen chico' – the good boy.
'El mal perro' – the bad dog.
If the noun is feminine, however, you must keep the 'a'. For example, 'The buena vista' – the good view.

> **[Spanish/English Difference] 'Thing'**
>
> When using conversational adjectives such as 'importante', 'interesante' or 'mejor' you may be tempted to add the word 'cosa' (thing) to make sentences such as 'La cosa importante.' You want to do this because in English you cannot use an adjective without a noun. In Spanish, however, you can and do use adjectives alone. The above example is completely wrong; it is instead 'lo importante.'
>
> 'Lo' has no equivalent in English but it precedes adjectives when we would use 'thing' or 'part'. For example:
>
> 'Lo importante es que sabes la repuesta' – the important thing is that you know the answer.
>
> 'Lo mejor de la película fue cuando él apareció' – the best part was when he appeared.
>
> 'Lo maravilloso es....' – the wonderful thing is...

Comparatives and superlatives

A comparative sentence compares two or more nouns. For example, 'Spain is bigger than Ireland,' 'Mumbai is less expensive than London' or 'playing football is more fun than doing your homework.'

In Spanish this is fairly simple; adjectives do not change as they do in English, everything is done with 'más' (more) or 'menos' (less), with a structure that runs:

Noun + ser + más (or menos) + adjective + que + noun

For example, the above sentences would be:

'España es más grande que Irlanda.'

'Mumbai es menos caro que Londres.'

'Jugar a fútbol es más divertido que hacer los deberes.'

Comparatives II: As and As

There are however, two ways to say a comparison in English. These are: 'France is bigger than Belgium' and 'Belgium is not as big as France.' Spanish does the same thing but instead of an 'as' + 'as,' its structure is:

No + ser + tan (so) + adjective + como (as)

The above sentence would be 'Bélgica no es tan grande como Francia,' (literally 'Belgium is not so big as France.')

More examples:
'Mi prima no es tan alta como mi hermana' – my cousin isn't as tall as my sister.
'Las naranjas no son tan caras como las piñas' –oranges aren't as expensive as pineapples.
'La rosa no crece tan rápido como el girasol' – the rose doesn't grow as fast as the sunflower.

> **[Spanish/English Difference] Comparatives with numbers**
>
> If the comparative is followed by a number, change the 'que' to a 'de.' For example:
> 'Sophie trabajó más de 25 días en navidad' – Sophie worked more than ten days at Chistmas.
> 'Carlos tiene más de 50 videojuegos'– Carlos has 50 more than 50 videogames.
> 'Hay menos de cinco casas que podamos permitirnos en esta ciudad' – there are fewer than five houses that we can afford in this city.
> Remembering the 'de' takes practice but, it's important as 'que' here is completely wrong.

Than ever

The phrase for 'better than ever' or 'more than ever' is mejor que nunca or más que nunca. For example:

'Comó está tú abuela?' Mejor que nunca' – How is your grandmother? Better than ever.

'Más que nunca el mundo se calienta más' – The world is getting warmer more than ever.

Superlatives

Superlatives express 'the most' of something –such as, 'the biggest', 'the poorest,' 'the most expensive,' or 'the least popular.'

To do this in Spanish you place **el, la, los or las before the noun + más (or menos) + adjective**

For example:

'La montaña más alta en el mundo es el Everest' – the highest mountain in the world is Mount Everest.'

'¿Quién es la persona más manitas que conoces?' – who is the handiest person you know?

'¿Cuál es la ciudad más grande de Europa?' – what is the biggest city in Europe?

Making adjectives superlative when there is no noun

If you want to use a superlative without the noun then you put 'el'or 'la' before the adjective depending on the gender of the noun you are referring to. If your sentence refers to another adjective (such as a feeling) use 'lo.'

For example:

'El más grande es el mio' – the biggest is mine.

'Conoces esa película? ¡Es la mejor!' – do you know that film? It's the best!

'Lo menos dificil es montar en bici' – the least difficult thing is to ride a bike.

Irregular adjectives in comparative and superlative

Just as in English, 'bueno' (good) and 'malo' (bad) are irregular.

Adjective	Comparative	Superlative
Bueno	mejor	el/la/lo mejor
Malo	peor	el/la/lo peor

In English these would be 'better', 'best' and 'worse', 'worst'. For example:
'Hacer ejercicio es mejor que ver la tele' – doing exercise is better than watching the TV.
'Lo mejor es no dejar tu trabajo hasta el final del día' – it's best not to leave your work until the end of the day.
'Fumar es peor que comer chocolate' – smoking is worse than eating chocolate.
'El verano pasado fue las peores vacaciones de mi vida' – last summer was the worst holiday of my life.

Adjectives advanced

[Spanish/ English Difference] 'How' with adjectives

Questions

Spanish doesn't use how + adjective to ask about a degree of size, temperature or time. Instead it uses **cuánto/a or cuántos/as + verb.** For example:
'¿Cuánto mide tu coche?' – How big is your car?
'¿A cuántos kilómetros está Valencia de Madrid?' – How far is Valencia from Madrid?

Statements

For 'how + adjective' sentences use **lo + adjective + que.** For example:
'No sabes lo feliz que estoy' – you don't know how happy I am.
'Veo lo importante que es' – I see how important it is.
'¿Comprendes lo fácil que es?' – do you understand how easy it is?

Exclamations

For exclamations use **qué + adjective**. For example:

'¡Qué divertida fue la excursion!' – how fun the trip was!

'¡Qué alta es tu hija!' – how tall your daughter is!

Note: These are not questions. how tall is your daughter? Is '¿Cuánto mide tu hija?'

A + adjective/noun

A + adjective (or sometimes a noun) describes how something happens. Examples include:

'Nos fuimos a escondidas' – we left by stealth/in secret.

'Elegimos la película a ciegas' – we chose the film blind.

'Está a medias' – it's half finished.

'Llegamos a oscuras' – we arrived in darkness.

'Nos conocimos al azar' – we met by chance/at random.

'Lleva la maleta a golpes' – she carries the suitcase bumping along the ground.

'Imprimo los libros a demanda' – I print the books on demand.

3. Possessives

Possessive adjectives

It could be said that Spanish is obsessed with plurals. Not content with making adjectives plural ('Las casas grandes' for example) it has to make the possessive plural also. For example, 'mi coche' changes to 'mis coches' for more than one car. The same is true for all the possessive adjectives:

	Singular	Plural
my	mi	mis
your	tu	tus
his	su	sus
her	su	sus
its	su	sus
our	nuestro/a	nuestros/as
your (plural)	vuestro/a	vuestros/as
their	su	sus

Notice that 'his', 'her', 'its' and 'their' all have the same possessive 'su'. For example, in the sentence 'su hija se llama Lucia,' it could be 'his', 'her' or 'their' daughter that is called Lucia.

Notice also that 'nuestro' and 'vuestro' change gender depending on the gender of the noun – 'nuestra casa es blanca', 'vuestra comida es buena', 'nuestro pueblo es pequeño', 'vuestro hijo es guapo.'

Whose bag is it anyway?

To ask a possessive question in English we use the interrogative pronoun 'whose'. In Spanish this is expressed with 'de quién.' For example:

'¿De quién es esta bolsa?' – whose bag is this? (or literally 'of whom is this bag?)

'¿De quién es este perrito?' – whose dog is this?

The answer to this question is also with 'de.' For example,'la bolsa es de mi hija,' – The bag is my daughter's, 'el perrito es de mi vecina,' –the dog is my neighbour's.

Possessive pronouns

In English these are 'mine', 'your', 'ours' and so on. They are used when we want to reorder the possessive sentence. For example, 'it is my sofa' or 'the sofa is <u>mine</u>.'

	Singular	**Plural**
mine	mío/mía	míos/mías
your	tuyo/tuya	tuyos/tuyas
his	suyo/suya	suyos/suyas
hers	suyo/suya	suyos/suyas
ours	nuestro/nuestra	nuestros/nuestras
yours (vosotros)	vuestro/vuestra	vuestros/vuestras
theirs/yours (usted)	suyo/suya	suyos/suyas

Like possessive adjectives, possessive pronouns are plural if you are speaking about more than one object –'Los libros son nuestros' or 'Las fotos son suyas.'

[Common mistakes] Gender

In Spanish all possessive pronouns change their gender depending on the gender of the object – not the gender of the person who owns it. For example, a female would say 'el coche es mío' and a male 'la camiseta es mía' (the t-shirt is mine).

[Common mistakes II] Getting confused with his, hers, and theirs.

Because 'his', 'hers' and 'theirs' are all the same pronoun, Spanish speakers do not usually use 'suyo/a' when referring to 'theirs'. Instead they use 'de ellos' such as 'el jardín es de ellos' or 'las chaquetas son de ellos.' If 'they' is all female then you say 'ellas.'

> **[Spanish/English Difference] El mio/ la mia**
>
> If you have been around Spanish speakers you may have heard 'el mío' or 'la tuya' and so on. But when do you use the article?
>
> Well, you use it when the possessive replaces the noun. For example, 'mi libro es más grande que el tuyo' – my book is bigger than yours. 'El tuyo' here substitutes 'book', the 'el' reinforces that it is yours (literally, 'the yours'). The article changes depending on the gender of the noun. 'Su carta es blanca, la mía es negra' – his letter is white, mine is black.
>
> You don't use it when the possessive is preceded by the verb 'ser'. For example: 'Este lápiz es mío, ése es tuyo' – this pencil is mine, that one is yours.'

[Important different alert] Omit the 'of'

While 'of' precedes the possessive pronoun in sentences such as 'he is a friend of mine,' there is no 'de' in the Spanish equivalent. Instead it is 'él es amigo mío', or 'ella es compañera tuya' – she is a colleague of yours or 'ellos son paisanos míos' – They are countrymen of mine.

And finally

In English you cannot place a noun after the possessive pronoun (for example 'that is mine bread' is impossible). Ninety percent of the time this is also the case in Spanish. However, if you are referring to another person or entity who you affectionately think of as your possession you can use noun + mío. The three use cases for this are:

'Amigo mío' – my friend (or literally 'mine friend').

'Hijo mío' or 'Hija mía' – my son or daughter.

'Dios mío' – my God.

4. Pronouns

Subject pronouns

Subject pronouns are as follows in Spanish.

I	yo
you (informal)	tú
you (formal)	usted
he	él
she	ella
it	lo/la/le
we	nosotros/nosotras
you (plural)	vosotros/vosotras
they/you (formal, plural)	ellos/ellas

With verbs they work like this. Note, however, you don't have to use them as the subject (I, you etc) is understood by the verb ending.

Interrogative pronouns

These form question sentences and are:

Qué – This is 'what' when paired with a noun such as:'¿qué hora es?' – What time is it? And 'how' when paired with an adjective, such as: '¡qué grande es tu perro!' – how big is your dog! (This is not a question but rather an exclamation).

Cuál and cuáles (in plural) – This is 'which.' BUT: Cuál is used in place of qué in all 'ser' questions unless the question is 'what is that?' (¿cuál es eso?').

Quién and quiénes (in plural) – This is 'who.' For example:

'¿Quién es tu jefe?' – Who is your boss?

'¿Quiénes son tus maestros?' – Who are your teachers?

Cuál versus qué

As stated above, if the question uses 'ser' then it is proceeded by 'cuál'- meaning that many questions that would start with 'what' in English actually start with 'which.' For example:

'¿Cuál es tu nombre?' – what is your name? (or which is your name?)

'¿Cuál es la fecha?' – what is the date?'

'¿Cuáles son las clases que te gustan?' – what are the classes you like?

In English, 'which,' is used to choose between a few options (usually, 10 or, fewer). Spanish does not use 'cuál' this way. In sentences without 'ser' the question is made with qué even if there are only a few options. For example:

'¿Qué planta quieres?' – which floor (in a building) do you want?

'¿Qué vaso prefieres? – which glass do you prefer?

'¿Qué libro me has dado, el rojo o el azul?' – which book have you given me, the red one or the blue one?

Other question words

Dónde – This is 'where'. This combines with 'a' to create 'to where' in direction questions. For example:

'Adónde vas?' – Where are you going? (Or literally, 'to where are you going?')

Cuándo – This is 'when.'

Por qué – This is 'why.'

Cómo – This is 'how.'

Why and Because

'Por qué' ('why') is easily confused with 'porque' ('because'); the two words conjoined and without an accent (quite literally, 'for what?')

The two are distinguished in speech by making the 'qué' sharper with 'why' ('por *qué*') and lengthening the 'or' part of 'because' to make 'p*or*que.'

Object pronouns

Object pronouns substitute the noun. In English these are 'me', 'him', 'her' and so on. For example, in the sentence 'Give Sam the pen,' Sam is a noun, which can be changed to 'Give her the pen.' In Spanish the pronoun either comes before the verb as a separate word or after, joined with the verb, and so the sentence. Note, however, that where you place the pronoun changes the meaning. When you place a pronoun before the verb you are describing an action when you place it after you are giving command. For example:

'Le da el boli' – he is giving her the pen.
'Dale el boli' – give her the pen.

Object pronouns in Spanish are:

	Direct object	**Indirect object**
me	me	me
you	te	te
him	lo/le	le
her	la	le
it	lo	le
us	nos	nos
you (informal, plural)	os	os
you (formal, plural)	los/las	les
them	los/las	les

Note: 'me' is pronounced 'meh.'
More examples include:
'Hazle tostadas' – make him some toast.
'Os llamo manaña' – I will call you tomorrow.
'Míralos jugando' – look at them playing.
'Les pása la sal' – he is passing them the salt.
'Pásales la sal' – pass them the salt.

Direct and indirect object pronouns

As you can see, object pronouns are a little more complicated in Spanish and that is because they change depending on whether you are referring to the direct or indirect object.

Direct and indirect objects are nothing to be afraid of – we have them in English.

How direct and indirect objects work

The majority of sentences have two objects. The direct object is the noun or pronoun on the receiving end of the action –for example, 'pass me the pen' – it is the pen here that is undergoing the action (by being passed around).

The indirect object is the person or entity *for* whom you are doing the action. In the above sentence the indirect object is 'me'. Another way to say this would be 'pass the pen *for* me'.

In English indirect objects are often indicated with the prepositions 'for' or 'to.' For example, 'explain the problem to us' – the problem is the direct object while 'us' is the indirect object. With pronouns this is 'explain it to us.'

In the Spanish equivalent of this sentence the direct object is signified with 'lo' and the indirect with 'nos.' So it would be 'explícanoslo' – the indirect object goes first followed by the direct (or in other words 'lo' and 'la' go at the end).

'Explain to him the problem' would be 'explícale el problema.' More examples:

'Dales las cartas' – give the letters to them ('cartas' are the direct object receiving the action while 'les' are the indirect object you are doing it for).

'Cómprale una manzana' – buy an apple for him.

'Les contó el cuento' – he told them the story.

'Le llevo una bolsa al colegio' – I am taking a bag to school for her.

The le, lo, la rule

If I were to say in Spanish 'Give them to them' I would end up with 'daleslas.' These are too many 'l' words for comfort. To avoid the repetition of all those 'l' sounds 'le' and 'les' change to 'se' when paired with 'lo,' 'la', 'los' or 'las.'

So the above sentence would be 'dáselas.' More examples:

'Explícaselo' – explain it to her.

'Préstaselo' –lend him/them it.

[Common mistakes I] Lo and le

So you have your direct and indirect objects down and are using 'lo' and 'le' like a pro. But there is just one problem, you're not.

In Spain 'lo' is not commonly used to refer to 'him' even if it is the direct object. Instead people use 'le'. For example, 'Le conozco desde hace muchos años' – I have known him for many years. 'Lo conozco,' is almost never used and so sounds incorrect to Spanish speakers (even though technically it is the right form to use).

Confusing though this may be, it actually makes life easier. People are hardly ever the direct object in sentences anyway as you almost never do something *to* a person but rather do something *for* them (making them the indirect object). This means that most of the time 'le' or 'les' is correct anyway.

Now if you always use 'le' for him the only thing you have to worry about is when to use 'la,' 'los' and 'las' which is only possible in a few cases, such as 'la veo', 'las conozco,' 'los llevo' and 'la recojo.'

For example a feminine direct object sentence would be:

'La llevo al colegio' – I take her to school.

A masculine equivalent would be:

'Le llevo al colegio' – I take him to school.

[Common mistakes II] Not using 'le' enough

'Le', 'les' and other indirect object pronouns are often placed before the verb and **a + prepositional pronouns** (mí, tí, él, ella and so on) after the verb to add emphasis about who the action is for. For example:

'Le mandé el paquete a ella' – I sent the package to her.

'Les propongo a ellos un solución' – I propose a solution to them.

Prepositional pronouns

These pronouns are used after prepositions, such as para, con or de. They are:

me	mí
you	ti
him	él
her	ella
us	nosotros
you (formal, singular)	usted
you (informal, plural)	vosotros
you (formal, plural)	ustedes
them	ellos/ellas

For example:

'Vivo cerca de ellos' – I live close to them.

'la comida es para ti – the food is for you. .

'La casa es para nosotros' – the house is for us.

'Voy al mercardo con vosotros' – I am going to the market with you.

Conmigo / contigo / consigo

'Con' is also commonly combined with 'mí' and 'ti' to make 'conmigo' (with me) and 'contigo' (with you). For example:

'Vienes conmigo?' – are you coming with me?

'Sí, voy contigo' – yes I am going with you.

There is also 'consigo' to mean 'with himself', 'with herself' or 'with themselves.' However, it is hardly used to mean 'with themsleves' as it is not clear who you are referring to. Instead, most people prefer to say 'con ellos' or 'con ellas.'

Relative pronouns

Relative pronouns connect two clauses together in a sentence – such as, 'the man who mows the lawn' or 'the pen which I use for work.'

In Spanish relative pronouns are 'que' (that), 'cual' and 'quien.' Unlike interrogative pronouns they do not contain accents.

Which pronoun do I use?

To understand which pronoun to use first we must take a moment to analyse relative clauses in English. Relative clauses are divided into two types; defining and non-defining.

In defining clauses, the clause is not separated from the rest of the sentence with commas. For example:

'The woman who teaches me French is called Sabine' or 'the shoes which you bought me are blue.'

In both these sentences 'who' (referring to a person) and 'which' (referring to a thing) can be substituted for 'that.'

'Que' is also the pronoun you use in Spanish: 'La mujer que me enseña francés se llama Sabine' and 'los zapatos que me compraste son azules.'

With non-defining clauses, the clause (which is often superfluous to the sentence) is removed from the rest of the sentence with commas. For example:

'Maria, who is my neighbour, is a really good singer.'

In English non-defining clauses must use 'who' for people and 'which' for things.

In Spanish, however, you use 'que' for non-defining clauses also. When referring to a person you could use 'quien' but this is optional.

For example, the above sentence would be:

'Maria, que es mi vecina, es muy buena cantante' or 'Juan, que es mi antiguo maestro , me ofreció un trabajo' – Juan, who is my old teacher, offered me a job.

El que, la que, los que, las que – that which or the one which

Before you get too excited, not every relative clause can be connected with just 'que.'

'El que', 'la que', 'los que' and 'las que' refer to a particular person or object. Their gender and quantity is reflected in the pronoun. In English this would be 'the one' or 'the one which.' For example:

If you want someone to pass you a pencil and you don't want just *any* one but rather the one closest, you would say:

'Pásame el que está más cerca' – pass me the one which is closest.

If you were talking about your neighbours and wanted to express precisely which one, you would say, '¿Sabes a quien me refiero? La que tiene el perro blanco' – do you know who I am speaking about? The one with the white dog.

When 'que' (that) becomes 'which' with prepositions

'El que', 'la que', 'los que' and 'las que' become 'in which' 'of which' and 'with which' with the prepositions 'en', 'de' and 'con.'

For example:

'La casa en la que vivimos es muy grande' – the house in which we live is very big (or 'the house which we live in is very big').

'Las clases de las que hablábamos ayer, empiezan mañana' – the classes of which we were speaking yesterday, start tomorrow (or 'the classes which we were speaking about yesterday start tomorrow').

'El ordenador con el que estudia está roto' – the computer with which he studies is broken (or 'The computer which he studies with is broken').

Lo que – what or which

If speaking about an idea or feeling then you use the neutral 'lo que.' In English this is 'what' or 'which.' For example:

'Él siempre quiere ver películas de acción, lo que me molesta' – he always wants to watch action movies, which annoys me.

'No escuché lo que estaba diciendo' – I didn't listen to what he was saying.

'Ellos no saben lo que quieren hacer en la vida' – they don't know what they want to do with their lives.

El cual, la cual, los cuales, las cuales
'El cual', 'la cual', 'los cuales', 'las cuales' can be used in place of 'el que', 'la que', 'los que' and 'las que'. However, these pronouns are old-fashioned and not commonly used.

When who becomes whom
'Whom' is used when a person is the object of a sentence. For example:
'The woman whom I love is coming to live with me.'
'Whom' sounds old-fashioned now and we hardly use it in English, but it is still essential in Spanish.
In Spanish 'who' becomes 'whom' when it is preceded by a preposition, most commonly 'con', 'de' or 'a'. For example:
'¿Con quién vas a la boda?' – with whom are you going to the wedding?
'¿De quién hablas?' – about whom are you speaking?
If there is no obvious preposition then you put 'a'. For example:
'Saludamos a Jorge a quien vimos jugando ayer en el parque' – we said hello to Jorge whom we saw playing in the park yesterday.
'El criminal a quien capturaron ayer había robado el banco' – the criminal whom was captured yesterday had robbed the bank.'

Cuyo/cuya and cuyos/cuyas – whose
'Whose' is the possessive pronoun – for example, 'Facebook, whose app is on my tablet, is a social networking site.'
In Spanish this would be 'Facebook, cuya aplicación está en mi tablet, es un sitio de redes sociales.'
'Cuyo' is 'whose' for masculine nouns while 'cuya' is for feminine. It is 'cuya' in the example above because 'whose' refers to 'aplicación,' which is feminine, and not 'Facebook'.

Other examples include:

'Mi madre, cuyo negocio va muy bien, acaba de vender su primer cuadro' – my mother whose business is doing very well, just sold her first painting.

'Nuestro vecino, cuya hija es médica, ha comprado un nuevo coche' – our neighbour whose daughter is a doctor has just bought a new car.

Alguien and algo – someone and something

Another pair of essential pronouns are 'alguien' (someone) and 'algo' (something). These are used with affirmative statements and questions. For example:

'¿Tienes algo de comer?' – do you have anything to eat?

'Tengo algo, pero no te gusta' – I have something, but you don't like it.

'¿Conoces a alguien francés?' – do you know anyone French?

'Sí, conozco a alguien' – yes I know someone.

Negatives

The negatives of these sentences would be with 'nada' (nothing or not anything) and 'nadie' (no one or not anyone). For example:

'No, no tengo nada de comer' – no, I don't have anything to eat.

'No tengo nada' – I have nothing.

'No, no conozco a nadie francés' – I don't know anyone French

Note that 'a' goes before 'nadie' in this case because you are referring to a person. This is known as the personal 'a.' For more information see the prepositions chapter.

Algún sitio – somewhere

'Somewhere' in Spanish is most commonly 'algún sitio' (although there are more variations). It is used for affirmative sentences and questions. For example:

'¿Conoces algún sitio donde pueda tomar un café?' – do you know anywhere where I can have a coffee?'

'Sí, conozco un sitio al fondo de la calle' – Yes, I know somewhere at the end of the street.

Negatives

The negative of this sentence would be with 'ningún sitio,' meaning 'nowhere' or 'not anywhere'. For example:

'No, no conozco ningún sitio donde puedas tomar un café' – no, I don't know anywhere where you can have a coffee.'

'No conozco ningún sitio' – 'I know nowhere.'

The whole someone, something, somewhere question can be summed up in this table:

	Affirmative	**Negative**	**Question**
someone/anyone	alguien	nadie	alguien
something/anything	algo	nada	algo
somewhere/anywhere	algún sito	ningún sitio	algún sitio

For more on alguno and ninguno go the Some, Any and Nothing chapter.

5. The present tense

The basics

Verbs in Spanish end in either -ar, -er or -ir. Take a look at these regular verbs in the following lists:

-ar		-er		-ir	
arreglar	to sort out	beber	to drink	abrir	to open
bajar	to go down	comer	to eat	compartir	to share
cocinar	to cook	correr	to run	cubrir	to cover
comprar	to buy	creer	to believe	decider	to decide
continuar	to continue	Leer	to read	descubrir	to discover
limpiar	to clean	romper	to break	escribir	to write
organizar	to organise	vende	to sell	subir	to go up
preparar	to prepare			vivir	to live
sacar	to take out			abrir	to open
trabajar	to work			compartir	to share

To change a root verb such as 'cocinar' ('to cook'), remove the -ar, -er, or -ir part of the verb and add an appropriate ending. This is called conjugating the verb and it works like this:

Cocinar (-ar verb)

Cocino – I cook

Cocinas – you cook (informal)

Cocina – he, she, it, you (formal) cooks

Cocinamos – we cook

Cocináis – you cook (plural, informal)

Cocinan – they cook or you cook (plural, formal)

Beber (-er verb)

Bebo – I drink

Bebes – you drink (informal)

Bebe – he, she, it, you (formal) cooks

Bebemos – we drink

Bebéis – you drink (plural, informal)

Beben – they drink or you drink (plural, formal)

Escribir (-ir verb)

Escribe – I write

Escribes – you write

Escribe – he, she it, you (formal) writes

Escribimos – we write

Escribis – we write

Escriben – they write or you write (plural, formal)

Note: You do not have to use the subject pronoun 'yo', 'tú', 'él', 'ella' and so on before the verb as the listener understands who is being referred to by the verb endings. Just in case you don't remember the subject pronouns here they are again with the verb 'leer' ('to read').

Yo leo – I read

Tú lees – you read

Él lee – he reads

Ella lee – she reads

Usted lee – you read (formal)

Nosotros leemos – we read (masculine)

Nosotras leemos – we read (feminine)

Vosotros leéis – you read (plural informal, masculine)

Vosotras leéis – you read (plural, informal, feminine)

Ellos leen – they read (masculine)

Ellas leen – they read (feminine)

Ustedes leen – you read (plural, formal)

Also: If you are referring to a group of both men and women then use the masculine forms ('ellos', 'nosotros' and 'vosotros').

Negatives and questions

Again, to make the verb negative put a 'no' before it.

For example:

'Como carne pero no como cerdo' – I eat meat but I don't eat pork.

'Mis padres leen los periódicos, pero no escriben mensajes de correo electrónico' – My parents read newspapers but they don't write emails.'

For questions, the sentence remains in its affirmative form and the speaker changes the intonation of their voice so that the listener understands it's a question.

Stem change and irregular verbs

Before you get too carried away with your new found language skills it is important to note that there is a long list of verbs in the present tense which are irregular. This is not done to trick language learners but rather to help the words flow smoothly off the speaker's tongue.

Take the verb 'querer' ('to want' or 'to love'). If you continued with the standard system 'I want' would be 'quero' which is awkward to say. To avoid this problem you instead change the verb to 'quiero' which is much easier to say. This is called a stem change and I will touch briefly on the six main ones below.

Ar and Er Verbs

When 'e' changes to 'ie': Typical verbs 'querer', 'pensar', 'entender'

As with 'querer' there are many verbs where the first 'e' changes to 'ie'. Look at the system below. All of these verbs end in -er or -ar.

E > ie

Pensar (to think)	Entender (to understand)
pienso	entiendo
piensas	entiendes
piensa	entiende
pensamos	entendemos
pensáis	entendéis
piensan	entienden

Note that with nosotros and vosotros there is no stem change.

Common verbs that follow this pattern:

-Ar		-Er	
acertar	to guess	defender	to defend
atravesar	to cross	descender	to descend
cerrar	to close	encender	to light up
comenzar	to start	perder	to lose
empezar	to begin	querer	to want
nevar	to snow		
recommender	to recommend		

When o changes to ue: Typical verbs volver, jugar, sonar

The next set of verbs changes the first 'o' or 'u' to 'ue'. All end in -ar or -er. Take a look below.

O -> ue	U -> ue
volver	jugar
vuelvo	juego
vuelves	juegas
vuelve	juega
volvemos	jugamos
volvéis	jugáis

vuelven	juegan

Again the verb in nosotros and vosotros form stays the same.

Common verbs that follow this pattern are:

-Ar		-Er	
acordarse	to remember	conmover	to move (emotion)
acostarse	to go to bed	devolver	to return (a thing)
aprobar	to approve	doler	to hurt
colgar	to hang up	llover	to rain
costar	to cost	morder	to bite
encontrar	to find	mover	to move
soñar con	to dream	oler	to smell
volar	to fly	poder	to be able to

NOTE: The verb 'oler' (to smell) is very irregular. For all present tense forms except for nosotros and vosotros, an 'h' precedes the word and so it is: 'yo huelo', 'tú hueles', 'él, ella huele', 'nosotros olemos', 'vosotros oléis' and 'ellos huelen'.

Ir verbs

Stem change verbs with 'ir' endings come in three categories.

When 'e' changes to 'ie'. Typical verbs: Pedir, sentir, mentir.

The second 'e' in the verb changes to 'ie' except in nosotros or vosotros form.

Preferir
prefiero
prefieres
prefiere
preferimos
preferís
prefieren

Common verbs that have this form:

advertir	to notify
convertir	to convert
divertirse	to have a good time
hervir	to boil
mentir	to lie
referir	to refer to
sentir	to regret
sentirse	to feel

When 'o' changes to 'ue.' Verbs: dormir and morir.

There are only two verbs that use this stem change. These are 'dormir' (to sleep) and 'morir' (to die). Note that again there is no stem change for nosotros and vosotros.

Dormir (to sleep)
duermo
duermes
duerme
dormimos
dormís
duermen

When 'e' changes to 'i'. Typical verbs: Pedir, seguir, vestir.

This is when the 'e' of the main verb changes to 'i'. This change is one of the hardest to master as the difference in pronunciation is small, but essential to learn. Take a look at the pattern below. As usual nosotros and vosotros remain the same.

Pedir (to ask for, to order)
pido

pides
pide
pedimos
pedís
piden

Common verbs that follow this pattern are:

despedir	to fire from a job
despedirse	to say goodbye
impeder	to avoid, impede
medir	to measure
perseguir	to pursue, follow
reírse de	to laugh at
repetir	to repeat
seguir	to follow, continue
server	to serve
sonreírse	to smile
vestirse	to get dressed

Verbs ending in uir. Typical verbs: incluir, destruir, sustituir.

With these verbs you change the 'uir' to 'y' before the conjugation except for nosotros and vosotros which remain the same. For example

Incluir (to include)
incluyo
incluyes
incluye
incluimos
incluís
incluyen

Note that verbs ending in 'guir' such as 'seguir' and 'perseguir' do not follow this pattern. Common verbs with this stem change include:

atribuir	to attribute
concluir	to conclude
contribuir	to contribute
destruir	to destroy
distribuir	to distribute
huir	to flee
influir	to influence
sustituir	to substitute

Verbs that are irregular in first person only

There is also a final list of verbs that are irregular only in the 'yo' form. These are:

caber (to fit)	quepo (I fit)
caer (to fall)	caigo (I fall)
dar (to give)	doy (I give)
estar (to be)	estoy (I am)
hacer (to do)	hago (I do)
poner (to put)	pongo (I put)
saber (to know)	sé (I know)
salir (to leave, go out)	salgo (I go out)
traer (to bring)	traigo (I bring)
valer (to be worth)	valgo (I value)
ver (to see)	veo (I see)

When is the present tense used in Spanish?

When you think about it, we hardly use the present in English. It is used for routines and giving orders and the majority of the time we use other tenses to express what is happening now, what will happen in the future and what has just happened. This is not the case in Spanish. All of these ideas (within reason) can be expressed with present. The present tense is used for:

Routines and habits. Just as in English if you want to talk about something that happens regularly you use present.
For example:
'Compro la comida los lunes' – I buy food on Monday.
'Al medio día yo y mis compañeros corremos en el parque' – at midday my companions and I run in the park.

To describe an action that is happening now. This is a crucial one; in English this would almost always be in the continuous tense ('I am playing football'). Though Spanish has a continuous tense also, it is not nearly as used.
For example:
'¿Juegas a fútbol con nosotros?' – are you playing football with us?
'¿Qué haces con esa pintura?' – what are you doing with that paint?
'Julio llega ahora y comemos' – Julio is arriving now and we will eat.
For more about the present versus the continuous tense take at The Continuous chapter.

To describe an event that will take place in the near future. Normally a future time marker is used for clarification.
For example:
'¿Te llamamos sobre este asunto mañana por la tarde, vale?' – we will call you about the issue tomorrow afternoon, ok?
'A este ritmo no acabo esta semana' – at this rate we won't finish it this week.
'En navidad mi familia me visita' – at Christmas my family will visit me.

For more about the present versus the future tense, take a look at The Future chapter.

To ask about a preference or permission (this can often be interpreted as shall):
'¿Pintamos la sala or el dormitorio primero?' – shall we paint the living room or the bedroom first?
'¿Juegas a fútbol o a tenis?' – do you play football or tennis?
'¿Te ayudo llevar los libros?' – shall I help you carry the books?

For something that started in the past and continues until now. In English this would be expressed with the present perfect tense – for example, 'I have known him for two years.' In Spanish you use present with the expression 'desde hace' to represent the time. For example:
'Le conozco desde hace dos años' – I have known him for two years.
'Vive aquí desde hace diez años' – she has been living here for ten years.
'Trabajan aquí desde hace cinco meses' – they have been working here for five months.

Time vocabulary
Hoy – today.
Manaña – tomorrow.
Esta semana – this week.
Este mes – this month.
Por la mañana – in the morning.
Por la tarde – in the afternoon.
Por la noche – at night.
El lunes, martes, etc - on Monday, Tuesday, etc.
Los lunes, los martes, etc – on Mondays, on Tuesdays, etc.
Note: There is no word for 'evening.' This is usually 'por la noche.'

6. Present tense questions and adverbs of frequency

Cuánto tiempo..? How long...?

The question 'how long...?' is **¿Cuánto tiempo hace que...?' + present tense.**
 For example:
'¿Cuánto tiempo hace que le concoces?' – how long have you known him for?
'¿Cuánto tiempo hace que vives aquí? – how long have you lived here for?

The other very common way to say 'how long' is **desde cuándo + present tense** (literally since when). For example:
'Desde cuándo trabaja para la empresa tu hermano?' – how long or Since when has your brother worked for the company for?
'Desde cuándo eres vegetariano?' – how long/ since when have you been a vegetarian?

Answering

Your answer to any of these questions would use **present + desde hace + time**. 'Desde hace' means 'for'. For example:
'Tenemos gato desde hace 10 años' – we have had a cat for 10 years.

Con qué frequencia/ how often

The question 'How often' is **con qué frequencia + present** in Spanish ('with what frequency?'). For example:
'¿Con qué frequencia haces la compra?' – how often do you go food shopping?
'¿Con qué frequencia va a la universidad tu hermana?' – how often does your sister go to the university?

Time clauses

The question can be answered with a time clause that goes at the end of the sentence, such as:

'Una vez a la semana' – once a week.

'Dos veces al mes' – two times a month.

'Tres veces al día' – three times a day.

'Cuatro veces al año' – four times a year.

If the noun is feminine – such as 'semana' you must use 'a' and 'la.' For example:

'Escucha la radio dos veces a la semana' – I listen to the radio twice a week.

If the noun is masculine you can combine 'a' and 'la' to make 'al.'

Adverbs of frequency

The other way to answer is with an adverb of frequency. These are:

- Siempre – always
- A menudo – often
- A veces – sometimes
- Casi nunca – hardly ever
- Nunca – never

They are placed either before or after the verb or at the end of the sentence. For example:

'Siempre me lavo los dientes dos veces al día' – I always brush my teeth twice a day.

'A veces ella va a correr por la mañana' – sometimes she goes running in the morning.

'Él no ordena casi nunca su cuarto' – he hardly ever tidies his room.

Note: Nunca and casi nunca can never go next to 'no'. For example, 'no nunca ordena su cuarto' is not correct.

'Van al cine a menudo' – he often goes to the cinema.

Desde/Since

If you want to answer with 'since' you use only 'desde.' For example:

'Soy vegetarian desde el principio del año' – I have been a vegetarian since the beginning of the year.

'Mi hermano trabaja para la empresa desde la universidad' – my brother has worked at the company since university.

Lleva + continuous

So far we have discussed the questions and answers for 'How long have you lived, worked, played…?' and so on but this is a very static and boring way to talk. In English a more normal question would be 'How long have you been living in London?' (for example).

Putting the verb into continuous emphasises the action to give you a livelier question. Likewise the most normal answer would be 'I have been living in London for two years' – also in continuous.

Spanish does the same thing with the verb **llevar + present continuous**.

'Llevar' normally means 'to take' (as in 'I will take you to the airport,' rather than 'take this pen') or 'to carry.' However, in this context it means 'have been.' For example:

'¿Cuánto tiempo llevas reparando mi coche?' – how long have you been repairing my car for?

'Llevo reparando tu coche 20 minutos' – I have been repairing your car for 20 minutes.

'¿Cuánto tiempo llevan casados?' – how long have they been married for?

'Pues, llevan casados 15 años' – well, they have been married for 15 years.

7. Gustar and back to front verbs

There is a list of verbs in Spanish that follow a different pattern which runs: Indirect object pronoun + verb in third person singular or plural. For example:
'Me gusta la fruta' – I like fruit (or literally, 'the fruit is liking me')
The concept 'fruit' is uncountable, and so 'gustar' is in singular. When the subject is plural it changes to 'gustan,' for example:
'Me gustan los plátanos' – I like bananas.
 'Le gusta el vino' – he likes wine.
'Le gustan los bombones' – he likes chocolates.

To add emphasise speakers often put 'a' + prepositional pronoun, so the whole structure works like this:
(A mí) me gusta –I like.
(A ti) te gusta – you like.
(A él) le gusta – he likes.
(A ella) le gusta – she likes.
(A usted) le gusta – you like.
(A nosotros) nos gusta – we like.
(A vosotros) os gusta – you like.
(A ellos/ellas) les gusta – they like.
(A ustedes) les gusta – they like.

With another verb
If you want to use another verb with 'gustar' you use the infinitive with no preposition.
'¿Te gusta cocinar?' – Do you like to cook?
'No, no me gusta cocinar' – No, I don't like to cook.

Saying how much you like something

You place any adverb to say how much or how little you like something directly after 'gustar' for example, 'Me gusta mucho pintar' – I like painting a lot.

Gustar in other tenses

Back to front verbs are in third person for all tenses. For example:
'Le gustó pintar con los niños' – he liked painting with the children.
'¿Te gustaría ir al cine?' – would you like to go to the cinema?

Other verbs that follow this pattern

Apetecer – to fancy
'¿Te apetece un café?' – do you fancy a coffee?

Doler – to hurt
'Le duele el abrazo' – his arm hurts or it hurts him, the arm.

Faltar – to lack
Nos faltan dos semanas mas hasta el fin del curso – we lack two more weeks until the end of the course, or there are two weeks left until the end of the course.

Encantar – to love
'Le encantó conocerte' – he loved meeting you.

Importar – to mind, matter
'No me importa tu perro' – I don't mind about your dog.

Interesar – to interest
'Los museos no me interesan mucho' – museums don't interest me much

8. Infinitives

Now, before we go on, I must mention infinitives. An infinitive is the root verb with no stem changes. In a sentence, the first verb makes the tense and changes depending on whether it is 'I', 'you', 'he', 'she' and so on. The verb that comes after that is the infinitive. For example:
'She likes to run' or 'he preferred to drink coffee without milk.'
In English the standard infinitive is preceded by the preposition 'to.' In Spanish there is no preposition, so the sentences above would be:
'A ella le gusta correr' and 'él prefirió beber café sin leche.'

> **[Spanish/English Difference] Infinitives**
> It is a common mistake among English speakers to try to squeeze in an 'a' (to) before an infinitive because that is how they are used to speaking. This mistake must be eliminated or your speech will always sound strange.

Common verbs that are not followed by an 'a'

Encantar – to love
'Os encanta salir los fines de semana' – you love to go out at the weekend.

Gustar – to like
'Les gusta tocar música con sus amigos' – they like to play music with their friends.

Intentar – to try
'Intento estudiar cada noche' – I try to study every night.

Necesitar – to need
'Necesitan saber la verdad' – they need to know the truth.

Preferir – to prefer
'Preferimos sentarnos fuera para comer' – we prefer to sit outside to eat.

Querer – to want

'Quiero saber más de tu cultura' – I want to know more about your culture.

Saber – to know how to

'Ella sabe bailar pero no sabe cantar' – she knows how to dance but she doesn't know how to sing.

When the verb does have a preposition

However, it is important to note that there is a list of verbs that are followed by 'a,' as well as other prepositions, because that is their structure.

Popular verbs with 'a' include:

Aprender a

Empezar a

Invitar a

Ir a

Venir a

Volver a

The infinitive with adjectives

Just like English, verbs are always in infinitive after adjectives, but, the infinitive in Spanish is without 'a'. For example:

'Es imposible estudiar a las tres de la madrugada' – it's impossible to study at three in the morning.

'Es difícil aprender a conducir a los 70 años' – it's difficult to learn to drive at 70 years old.

'Es divertido bailar en la playa' – it's fun to dance on the beach.

The infinitive after prepositions

Prepositions are words such as 'de' (from, of), 'en' (on, in) and 'entre' (between, among). There are many more and they give information about what, where, when and why something takes place. For more information see The Prepositions chapter.

In English verbs after prepositions change from infinitive to gerund form by adding an 'ing' at the end. In Spanish they remain a straight infinitive.
For example:
'Tengo miedo de volar' – I am scared of flying.
'Me preocupo por aprobar mi examen' – I worry about passing my exam.
'Estoy pensando en ir a Francia por las vacaciones' – I am thinking about going to France for my holidays.
You'll notice that the verbs in the last two sentences carry different prepositions than their English equivalents. There is a small but important list of verbs that are like this – see The Prepositions chapter.

The infinitive at the beginning of sentences
In English, verbs that start a sentence are in gerund form (ending in 'ing'). In Spanish they remain in normal infinitive. For example:
'Hacer ejercicio es bueno para la salud' – doing exercise is good for your health.
'Comprar una casa requiere mucho dinero hoy en día' – buying a house requires lots of money nowadays.

Infinitives advanced

De + infinitive
'De' can also be translated as 'to'. Its job is to show what the subject of the sentence does. It is always followed by the infinitive. For example:
'Una cámara de sacar fotos' – 'camera' is the subject and so it is 'a camera to take photos.'
If you add a person to this sentence they become the subject and the camera the object, so 'de' changes to 'para' to refer to what the camera does *for* me.
'Tengo una camera para sacar fotos' – I have a camera to take photos.
'Un cuchillio de cortar pan es mejor que uno normal' – a knife for bread is better than a usual one.

9. Obligation, ability and deduction

Obligation: Must, have to, should

In English strong obligation is expressed with 'must' and 'have to,' and mild obligation with 'should'. Spanish expresses similar ideas with the following verbs.

Deber – must

This is a regular verb that follows the pattern:

Debo – I must.

Debes – you must.

Debe – he, she, it must.

Debemos – we must.

Debéis – you (plural) must.

Deben – they must.

For example:

'Debo ir al médico' – I must go to the doctor.

'Debes estudiar esta noche' – You must study tonight.

Negatives: Mustn't

'Mustn't,' which means prohibition, takes the form of 'no deber' –for example:

'No debes fumar aquí' – you mustn't smoke here.

'No deben comer chocolate cada día' – they mustn't eat chocolate every day.

Tener – to have

'Tener' works in the same way as English and means strong obligation (as well as possession). For example:

'Tengo que comprar más zapatillas' – I have to buy more trainers.

'Él tiene que hacer los deberes' – he has to do his homework.

Note that after tener you put 'que' before the infinitive (this would be 'to' in English).

Negatives: Don't have to

To make a 'don't have to' sentence to express 'no obligation' simply put a 'no' in front of 'tener.' For example:

'Ella no tiene que trabajar esta semana' – she doesn't have to work this week.

'No tenemos que vender el coche, ya tengo el dinero' – we don't have to sell the car, I already have the money'

Debería – should

Debería is the conditional of deber (literally 'would must'). Its closest equivalent in English is 'should'. Its conjugation runs:

Debería – I should.

Deberías – you should.

Debería – he, she, it should.

Deberíamos – we should.

Deberíais – you (plural) should.

Deberían – they should.

Negatives: Shouldn't

To make 'shouldn't' put a 'no' in front of the verb.

For example:

'No deberíamos tirar piedras' – we shouldn't throw stones.

'No deberías pelear con tu hermana' – you shouldn't fight with your sister.

Hay que + infinitive

This literally means 'one must' and is used to make general statements about what should be done in general rather than speaking about any individual in particular.

For example:

'Hay que hablar si quieres aprender otro idioma' – one must speak if one wants to learn other languages.

'Hay que hacer ejercicio si quieres estar en forma' – one must do exercise if one wants to be fit.

Negatives: Mustn't

The negative can mean both 'mustn't' and 'no need to.'

'No hay que conducir rápido en la carretera' – one mustn't drive fast on the highway.

'No hay que terminar el trabajo esta semana' – there is no need to finish the work this week.

Ability: Poder, podria

Poder – To be able to

'To be able to' ('can') is the irregular verb poder. Its conjugation runs:

Puedo – I can.

Puedes – you can.

Puede – he, she, it can.

Podemos – we can.

Podeís – you (plural) can.

Pueden – they can.

Poder works in the same way as 'can' in English. To make 'can't,' put a 'no' in front of the verb. For example:

'Puedo venir el sábado pero no puedo quedarme mucho' – I can come on Saturday but I can't stay long.

'¿No puedes contestar el telefóno? Sigue sonando.' – Can't you answer the telephone? It keeps ringing.

> **[Spanish/English difference] Poder is not used for knowledge**
>
> There is a small but significant difference between the meanings of 'can' and 'poder'. Though 'poder' does mean 'to be able to do something,' it does not mean 'to have the knowledge to do something.' This would be expressed instead with the verb 'saber' ('to know how to'). For example:
>
> '¿Sabes nadar?' – can you swim? (or 'do you know how to swim?')
>
> 'Yo sé montar en bici pero no sé montar en moto' – I can ride a bike but I can't ride a motorbike (or 'I know how to ride a bike, but I don't know how to ride a motorbike.')
>
> **[Spanish/English difference] Poder is not used with 'oír' (to hear) or 'ver' (to see)**
>
> While in English you would say 'can you see the mountain?' you do not use 'poder' this way in Spanish. Instead you say '¿ves la montaña?' or 'do you see the mountain?'
>
> The same is true for 'oír', for example:
>
> '¿Oyes el ruido del tráfico?' – can you hear the traffic noise? (Or 'do you hear the traffic noise?')
>
> 'No, no lo oigo, pero oigo tu perrito ladrando' – no, I can't hear it but I can hear your dog barking.

Podría – could

'Could' as in 'Could you pass me the salt' rather than the past tense of 'can' is 'Podría.' This is the conditional tense and runs:

Podría – I could.

Podrías – you could.

Podría – he, she, it could.

Podríamos – we could.

Podríais – you (informal) could.

Podrían – they could.

Like 'could', 'podría' is used as a polite way to ask for something or offer an idea.

For example:

'¿Podrías comprarme pan de la panadería?' – could you buy me some bread from the bakery?

'Podríamos visitar a tu familia este fin de semana o podríamos ver un partido de fútbol' – we could visit your family this weekend or we could see a football match.

Making deductions: Must be, should be

There is a difference between the statement: 'she must do her homework' and 'she must be a policewoman.'

The first is obligation, while the second, after taking account of the evidence; a uniform, a certain type of car and so on, deduces the profession this woman must have.

The second statement is a deduction and it is made with the same verbs ('deber' and 'debería') in Spanish as it is in English. In Spanish, however, speakers make the distinction by adding a 'de' after debe or debería, followed by the infinitive. For example:

'Debe de estar cansado, no suele dormir en el sofá' – he must be tired, he doesn't usually sleep on the sofa.

'Deben de estar organizados, tienen mucho éxito' – they must be organised, they are very successful.

'La cartera debería de estar en el coche, donde la dejaste' – the wallet should be in the car where you left it.

'Éste debe de ser el 10 de octubre' – this must be the 10th of October.

Negatives: No debe, no deben

In English the negative of 'he must be tired' would be 'he can't be tired' changing 'must' to 'can't'. In Spanish there is no verb change, you simply put 'no' in front of 'deber' or 'debería.' For example:

'No debe de ser rico, duerme en la calle' – he can't be rich, he sleeps in the streets.

'No deberían de estar malitos, estaban corriendo en el parque esta mañana' – they can't be (shouldn't be) sick, they were running in the park this morning.

Possibility: May and might

There are many ways to express 'may' and 'might' in Spanish. Unfortunately for students, because these sentences express doubt, the verb after the possibility is almost always in the subjunctive form which means that the stem changes. For more see The Subjunctive chapter.

Sentences that are not subjunctive are called indicative. If you want to avoid the subjunctive and still say 'I might go to the cinema this afternoon' then use 'a lo mejor' + verb in indicative form. For example the above sentence would be:

'A lo mejor voy al cine esta tarde.'

More examples:

'A lo mejor ella no quiere hacerse médico' – maybe she doesn't want to become a doctor.

'A lo mejor deberíamos irnos, el autobús sale pronto' – maybe we should go, the bus leaves soon.

May and might + subjunctive

If you want more options for 'may' and 'might' then you must learn the subjunctive tenses. The 'maybe' goes at the front of the sentence followed by the verb in present subjunctive, which refers to the present or the future.

Options include:

Quizá + subjunctive or indicative (depending on the situation) – perhaps.

'Quizá no coma carne' – perhaps he doesn't eat meat.

Tal vez + subjunctive or indicative (depending on the situation) – maybe.

'Tal vez no sepan de la situación' – maybe they don't know about the situation.

Puede que + subjunctive – may/might.

'Puede que haya una tormenta en China esta noche' – there might be a storm in China tonight.

Es posible que + subjunctive – it's possible that.

'Es posible que bebamos demasiado alcohol' – it's possible that we drink too much alcohol.

Es probable que + subjunctive – it's probabe that.

'Es probable que apruebe los exámenes' – it's probable that he will pass his exams.

10. Giving orders: The imperative tense

When giving orders English and Spanish speakers use the imperative tense. In English, this is the root verb without the subject ('take this paper', for example).

We use the imperative to soften the sentence. For example, you wouldn't say 'you give me this pen' – the 'you' makes it a harsh and offensive. However, it is perfectly acceptable to say 'give me this pen' particularly if you add a 'please' at the end. Omitting the subject pronoun ('you' in this case) softens the command.

The same happens in Spanish. You wouldn't say:

'Tú, dame el boli.' – 'you give me the pen.'

You would say:

'Dame el boli' – 'give me the pen.'

How to make an imperative

To create an imperative when speaking to an individual, change the verb into the third person. The object pronoun goes directly after the verb. More examples:

'Mírame' – look at me.

'Ayúdale' – help him.

'Pásales el pan' – pass them the bread.

Giving commands to more than one person

If you wish to give a command to a group of people then you must use a new verb conjugation. This is 'ad' for verbs that end in –ar, 'id' for –ir verbs and 'ed' for -er verbs. Take a look at this table:

Ar verbs	Imperative single	Imperative plural
Hablar	habla	hablad

pasar	pasa	pasad
llevar	lleva	llevad
trabajar	trabaja	trabajad

Ir verbs	Imperative single	Imperative plural
escribir	escribe	escribid
abrir	abre	abrid
vivir	vive	vivid

Er verbs	Imperative single	Imperative plural
beber	bebe	bebed
comer	come	comed
aprender	aprende	aprended

For example:

'Comed las patatas' – you (lot) eat the potatoes.

'Llevad esto a correos' – you (lot) take this to the post office.

'Aprended estos verbos este fin de semana' – you (lot) learn these verbs this weekend.

Negatives

This is where it gets tricky; Spanish has a whole other tense called the subjunctive that English doesn't have. The subjunctive is used to cast doubt on something, making the sentence more polite. You use this tense for negative imperatives. When you think about it, 'look at me' is a far more polite sentence than, 'don't look at me' which is why Spanish speakers add that extra level of politeness with the subjunctive. The subjunctive works like this:

-ar verbs

To create a third person singular conjugation, remove the 'a' and add an 'es'.

For example with the verb 'hablar':

Positive imperative: 'habla conmigo' – speak to me.

Negative imperative: 'no hables conmigo' – don't speak to me.

-er and –ir verbs

To create a third person singular conjugation, remove the 'e' and add 'as'.

For example, with the –er verb 'aprender':

Positive imperative: 'aprende otros idiomas' – learn other languages.

Negative imperative: 'No aprendas palabrotas' – don't learn swear words.

With the –ir verb 'abrir'

Positive imperative: 'abre la puerta' – open the door.

Negative imperative: 'No abras el cajón' – don't open the draw.

Note that these subjunctive stem changes are for regular verbs only. For check out our free accompanying book 'Spanish for Geniuses: verbs, prepositions and beginner vocabulary'.

Negative imperatives in plural

Plural negatives are made from the vosotros form of the verb changing the 'a' in –ar verbs to 'e' and the 'e' and 'i' in –er and -ir verbs to 'a'. For example:

Organizar – to organise

'No organizeis la fiesta, lo haré yo misma' – don't organise the party, I will organise it myself.

Beber – to drink

'No bebáis el agua, está mal hoy' – don't drink the water, it's bad today.

Escribir – to write

'No escribáis en la pared' – don't write on the wall.

Irregular imperatives

There are also a few imperatives that are irregular in singular form. These are:

Verb	Imperative
decir	di
hacer	haz
ir	ve
poner	pon
salir	sal
ser	sé
tener	ten
venir	ven

11. The future

Just like in English, there are several ways to say the future in Spanish, all of which we will cover in the following chapter.

Ir a – going to

The easiest way to express the future is by using the word 'ir'. Spanish speakers use 'ir' for future in the same way we use 'to go' but in the present tense instead of continuous. 'Ir' is an irregular verb that runs:

Yo voy – I go.

Tú vas – you go.

Él, ella, eso va – he, she, it goes.

Usted va – you (formal) go.

Nosotros vamos – we go.

Vosotros vais – you (plural, informal) go.

Ellos van – They or you go.

Ustedes van – You (plural, formal) go.

To express the future you use **'ir' in present + a + infinitive**. For negatives you simply put 'no' before the verb. For example:

'Voy a ir al supermercado' – I am going to go to the supermarket.

'Ella no va a la fiesta' – She isn't going to the party.

'Esta tarde vamos a jugar a fútbol y luego a ver a nuestra abuela' – this afternoon we are going to play football and then see our grandmother.

It is important to note that while 'going to' in English expresses a prearranged trip or plan (as opposed to 'will,' which expresses a more unpredictable future), Spanish makes no such distinction. You can use it for things that you can predict with some certainty will happen and those which you feel will only probably happen.

For example:

'Voy a ir la casa de mi abuela y le llevaré chocolate...' – I am going to go to my grandmother's house and bring her chocolate...

'...y se lo va a comer todo' – ...and she will eat it all.

Will

The second type of future in English is 'will.' Its closest equivalent in Spanish is the future tense, which is formed by attaching an ending to the infinitive verb. The endings are the same whether the verb ends in -ar, -er or -ir. They are:

Hablar	Pedir	Volver
hablaré	pediré	volveré
hablarás	pedirás	volverás
hablará	pedirá	volverá
hablaremos	pediremos	volveremos
hablaréis	pediréis	volveréis
hablarán	pedirán	volverán

Irregular verbs

There are a few irregular verbs in future. These are:

Verbs like poner ('to put'): For these verbs drop the 'e' or 'i' and add 'dr' + future.

Pondré, pondrás, pondrá, pondremos, pondréis, pondrán.

Other verbs with the same structure:

Salir – saldré.

Tener – tendré.

Valer – valdré

Venir – vendré.

Verbs like 'saber' ('to know'): For these verbs drop the vowel of the infinitive and add the future. Sabré, sabrás, sabra, sabremos, sabréis, sabrán.

Other verbs with the same structure include:

Caber – cabré

Haber – habré

Poder – podré

Querer – querré

Completely irregular verbs

Decir ('to say') and hacer ('to do') are completely irregular:

Decir: Diré, dirás, dirá, diremos, diréis, dirán.

Hacer: Haré, harás, hará, haremos, haréis, harán.

When to use to the future tense

It sounds obvious but the future tense in Spanish is used to talk about something that will happen in the future. In most cases this actually means the distant future.

For example:

'El año que viene cambiaré de trabajo' – next year I will change my job.

'Quedaremos el proximo mes para terminar la reunión' – we will meet next month to finish the meeting.

'En 10 años serán ricos' – in 10 years they will be rich.

It is also used for a prediction in either the present or the future. For example:

'El pronóstico dice que nevará mañana' –the forecast says that it will snow tomorrow.

'Él se cree que Madrid ganará la liga' – he thinks that Madrid will win the league.

'No sacarán buenas notas este año porque no han estudiado' –they probably won't get good results this year because they haven't studied.'

Typical time expressions with future:

Here are some time expressions commonly used with the future tense.

A la una o a las dos de la tarde – at one or at two in the afternoon.

El año que viene – next year.

El domingo que viene – next Sunday.

En un mes – in a month.

En una semana – in a week.

Esta noche – tonight.

Este verano – this summer.

Esta tarde – this afternoon.

Luego – later.

Mañana – tomorrow.

Mañana por la mañana – tomorrow morning.

Mañana por la tarde – tomorrow afternoon.

Pasado mañana – the day after tomorrow.

[Spanish/English Difference] When not to use the future

There are many cases in English we use 'will,' when in Spanish it would be present tense. These are:

1. An offer of help: For example:

'I'll take you to the airport', 'he'll open the door for you', 'will you call her?'

In these cases 'will' does not mean the future but rather expresses that you are willing to help (think of the sentence 'he'll open the door' – it is happening at this moment).

In Spanish this would be expressed in present.

Translations for the above examples:

'Te llevo al aeropuerto', 'te abre la puerta', '¿le llamas?'

2. An intention: For example:

'I will go to the supermarket this afternoon, if I have time', 'We will see each other tomorrow if you are not working', 'I will do my Spanish exam in the summer if I have improved.'

In these cases 'will' is not a concrete plan but rather an intention if other factors work out, allowing it to happen. The second half of the sentence (beginning with 'if') is either spoken or already understood. You could just say 'I will go to the supermarket this afternoon' and everyone will know that this is an intention that will probably happen, but is not set in stone.

The most common way to say this in Spanish is in present. With the above examples:

'Voy al supermercado esta tarde si tengo tiempo', 'nos vemos mañana si no trabajas', 'Si mejoro mi español, este verano me presento al examen.'

12. The conditional tense

The conditional is 'would' or 'could' in English. It is formed by adding ía to the end of the verb. Here are some examples with an -ar, -er and -ir verb.

Guarder (to keep)	Creer (to believe)	Traducir (to translate)
guardaría	creería	traduciría
guardarías	creerías	traducirías
guardaría	creería	traduciría
guardaríamos	creeríamos	traduciríamos
guardaríais	creeríais	traduciría
guardarían	creerían	traducirían

Irregular verbs in the conditional

Verbs that are irregular in future are also irregular in the conditional. To conjugate, make the verb into future, take away the last vowel and add -ía. Take a look at this list:

Present	Future	Conditional
caber	cabré	cabría
decir	daré	daría
haber	habré	habría
hacer	haré	haría
poder	podré	podría
querer	querré	querría
salir	saldré	saldría
saber	sabré	sabría
tener	tendré	tendría
valer	valdré	valdría
venir	vendré	vendría

The uses of the conditional tense

Hypothetical sentences

Just as in English, in Spanish you can use the conditional to communicate something that may happen in the present or future. For example:

'Maria dijo que prepararía la comida' – Maria said she would prepare the food.

'No caminaría en el bosque por la noche' – I wouldn't walk in the woods at night.

'Ella viviría en otro país pero no cambiaría su rutina' – she would live in another country but she wouldn't change her routine.

'Podríamos comprar otra tele, ésta es muy antigua' – we could buy another TV, this one is very old.

If clauses

The conditional is also used in conjunction with the past subjunctive to form an 'if' clause. For example:

'Si vinieras conmigo al baile, iría contigo al festival' – If you came with me to the dance, I would go with you to the festival.

'Podría tomar un café con ella si salieras con mi hermano una noche' – I could have a coffee with her if you went out with my brother one night.

For more on 'if' clauses see The subjunctive in past chapter.

Being Polite: Podría and Gustaría

Just as in English, you use 'podría' (could) and 'gustaría' (would like) to convey politeness. 'Gustaría' works in exactly the same way as gustar:

Indirect object pronoun (le, les and so on) + **gustaría** (for singular items) or **gustarían for plural** + **infinitive.** For example:

'Me gustaría tener dos niños' – I would like two children.

'¿Te gustaría tomar un café? – would you like to have a coffee?

'Le gustaría ir a Italia pero no me gustaría ir en avión' – he would like to go to Italy but I wouldn't like to fly (go by plane).

Podría is also + infinitive. For example:

'¿Podrías pasarme un sacapuntas?' – could you pass me a pencil sharpener?

'No podría comer patatas cada día, pero mi hermano podría' – I couldn't eat potatoes every day but my brother could.

Be careful: 'Could' in English means the conditional and the past, so when constructing sentences make sure you don't use 'podría' when you actually meant 'podía' (was able to) or 'pudo' (could in past).

13. The past

The preterite

The simple past in Spanish is known as 'el pretérito' and expresses an action that happened in the past that is now finished. For example:

'Ella llamó a su madre ayer para desearle feliz cumpleaños' – she called her mother yesterday to wish her happy birthday.

'Compraron el coche hace veinte años y aún funciona' – they bought the car twenty years ago and it still works.

It is, however, only the first of several past tenses, all of which I will go into in this book.To form the preterite you take away the -ar, -er and -ir from the infinitive and add the below endings.

Comprar (to buy)	Describir (to discribe)	Beber (to drink)
compré	describe	bebí
compraste	describiste	bebiste
compró	describió	bebió
compramos	describimos	bebimos
comprasteis	describisteis	bebisteis
compraron	describieron	bebieron

NOTE: The -ar and -ir verbs have the same ending as the present in the 'nosotros' form. However, it changes in -er form.

Irregular verbs in the preterite

Andar (to walk): anduve, anduviste, anduvo, anduvimos, anduvisteis, anduvieron

Estar (to be): estuve, estuviste, estuvo, estuvimos, estuvisteis, estuvieron

Dar (to give): di, diste, dio, dimos, disteis, dieron

Tener (to have): tuve, tuviste, tuvo, tuvimos, tuvisteis, tuvieron
Caber (to fit): cupe, cupiste, cupo, cupimos, cupisteis, cupieron
Poder (to be able to): pude, pudiste, pudo, pudimos, pudisteis, pudieron
Ponder (to put): puse, pusiste, puso, pusimos, pusisteis, pusieron
Saber (to know): supe, supiste, supo, supimos, supisteis, supieron
Ser and ir (to be, to go): fui, fuiste, fue, fuimos, fuisteis, fueron
Ver (to see): vi, viste, vio, vimos, visteis, vieron

NOTE: 'Saber' and 'caber' are almost never used in the preterite tense. It is much more common to use them in the imperfect tense. See The Imperfect below.

What is the preterite used for?
Spanish speakers use the preterite to express:
1. Something that happened in the past and is finished.
'Él habló con su profesora ayer pero no mencionó el problema' – he spoke to his teacher yesterday but he didn't mention the problem.

2. Something that happened at a particular moment and is now complete.
'La semana pasada comencé mi nuevo trabajo pero no vi a mií antigua amiga' – last week I started my new job but I didn't see my old friend.

Typical time phrases used with the preterite include:
Anoche – last night.
Anteanoche – the night before last.
Anteayer – the day before yesterday.
Ayer al mediodía – yesterday .
Ayer por la mañana – yesterday in the morning.
Ayer por la tarde – yesterday afternoon.
Ayer por la noche – yesterday night.

El año pasado – last year.

El lunes pasado – last Monday.

La semana pasada – last week.

El mes pasado – last month.

Hace diez años – ten years ago.

The imperfect

The next past tense is the imperfect. This tense expresses a repetitive or ongoing action in the past. In English this is expressed by 'used to' (as in 'I used to swim every day') or the past continuous ('I was studying all day yesterday'). The imperfect is very popular in Spain and is often used more then the preterite, possibly because the conjugation of the verb is much more simple.

-Ar verbs

For -ar verbs, take away the ending and add 'ba' in a system that runs like this:

Hablar (to speak)
hablaba
hablabas
hablaba
hablábamos
hablabais
hablaban

That's right, the 'yo', 'él', 'ella' and 'usted' forms are the same.

-Er and -ir verbs

For -er and -ir verbs, take away the ending and add ía. For example:

Vender (to sell)	Compartir (to share)
vendía	compartía
vendías	compartías
vendía	compartía
vendíamos	compartíamos
vendíais	compartíais
vendían	compartían

Irregular verbs

Irregular verbs in the imperfect are 'ir', 'ser' and 'ver.'

Ir (to go)	Ser (to be)	Ver (to see)
iba	era	veía
ibas	eras	veías
iba	era	veía
íbamos	éramos	veíamos
ibais	erais	veíais
iban	eran	veían

When is the imperfect used in Spanish?

The imperfect describes an ongoing or repeated action in the past.

The closest equivalent of the imperfect in English is 'used to', for example:

'Vivía en Madrid' – I used to live in Madrid.

'Él jugaba a fútbol cuando era joven' – he used to play football when he was young.

[Spanish/English Difference] The Imperfect

The first one is that while in English the first verb would start with 'used to' the second or third verbs would be in simple past. In Spanish, however, if you start with the imperfect to describe a repeated action you continue with that tense. For example:

'Cuando trabajaba para esa empresa tenía muchos compañeros de trabajo y pasabamos las fines de semana juntos' – when I used to work for that company, I had lots of workmates and we spent the weekends together. (Or literally, 'when I used to work for that company, I used to have lots of workmates and we used to spend the weekends together').

'Ellos compraban más verduras cuando eran vegeterianos y hacían más ejercicio' – they used to buy more vegetables when they were vegetarian and they did more exercise, (or literally, 'they used to buy more vegetables when they were vegetarians and they used to do more exercise').

The second important difference is that while 'used to' in English means you did something repeatedly in the past but now you don't, the imperfect could mean that you both used to do something and you still do. For example:

'Era un hombre muy honrado'

Translated literally this would be, 'he used to be a very honest man,' which implies that he is no longer honest. The imperfect doesn't work like this. Instead you are saying 'he was a very honest man over a long duration.'

More examples:

'Mis padres tenían mucho dinero' – my parents had a lot of money (over a long duration), not 'they used to have.'

'Era una época muy dura cuando nadie tenía mucho trabajo' – it was a very hard time, when nobody had much work.' Not 'It used to be a very hard time...' which implies that it's finished and everything is better now. In the above sentence, it could still be difficult now.

If you want to use the true translation of 'used to' to say that something did happen repeatedly but doesn't anymore, use 'antes' before the sentence.

> For example:
> 'Antes me gustaba nadar, pero ahora prefiero hacer yoga' – I used to like swimming but now I prefer to do yoga (i.e. 'I don't like swimming anymore').
> 'Antes odiaba a mi hermano pero ahora nos llevamos muy bien' – I used to hate my brother but we now get on really well.

Other uses of imperfect

The imperfect is also used to express doing something over a long duration. In English this would be expressed with the past continuous. For example:
'Estudiaba todo el fin de semana' – I was studying all weekend.
'Cuando vivía en Paris, visitaba mi panadería favorita cada día' – when I was living in Paris, I used to visit my favorite bakery every day.
'Los niños veían la tele mientras los padres limpiaban la casa' – the children were watching TV while the parents cleaned (were cleaning) the house.

Ser in imperfect (era)

'Era' is very common in speech as it describes the permanent qualities of someone or something in past tense. This could be the past as in 'yesterday' ('era un día hermoso' – it was a beautiful day) or the past as in the duration of a life ('la mujer era francesa' – the woman was French). More examples:
'Era una familia muy respetable' – they were a very respectable family.
'Era un coche muy cómodo' – it was a very comfortable car.
'Era una mujer muy guapa pero no era de nuestro pueblo, era de las montañas' – she was a very beautiful woman but she wasn't from our town, she was from the mountains.

When the imperfect is always used for past

Age: The imperfect is always used for age in past. Remember this is with 'tener' to express the amount of years and 'ser' for whether the person was old, young, a teenager or a child.

'Cuando tenía 18 años ella compró su primero coche' – when she was 18 years old she bought her first car.

'Cuando éramos joven, éramos muy delgados' – when we were young we were very slim.

Time: It is also used to indicate a time of day in the past.

'Eran las cinco de la tarde cuando llamaron' – it was at five in the afternoon when they called.

'¿Qué hora era cuando hablamos la última vez?' – when time was it when we last spoke?

To describe the background of a story: This is often found in literature, but it is used for speech also.

'Era un día bonito cuando Juan salió de casa' – it was a beautiful day when Juan left his house.

Typical time phrases used with the imperfect include:

A menudo – often.

A veces – sometimes.

Casi siempre – almost always.

De vez en cuando – from time to time.

Mientras – while.

Todas las mañanas – every morning.

Todos los años – every year.

Todos los días – every day.

Questions: How long + imperfect

In Spanish the question, 'How long have you been...?' is made with:

Cuánto tiempo hace que + present

For example:

'¿Cuánto tiempo hace que trabajas aquí?' – how long have you been working here.

To ask the question 'How long had you been...?' the structure is:

Cuánto tiempo hacía que' + verb in imperfect

Or

Hacía cuánto tiempo que' + verb in imperfect

For example:

'¿Cuánto tiempo hacía que trabajabas aquí antes de conocer a tu mujer?' – how long had you been working here before you met your wife?

The answer would also be in imperfect with the structure:

Hacía + expression of time + que + verb in imperfect

Or

Verb in imperfect + desde hacía + expression of time

For example:

'Hacía seis meses que trabajaba aquí antes de conocer a mi mujer' – I had been working here for six months before I met my wife.

'Iba a la clase de cerámica desde hacía dos meses antes de darme cuenta de que no me gustaba' – I had been going to my pottery class for two months before I realised I didn't like it.

However, if you want to express a past event that took place at a specific time ('ago' in English) use the preterite tense with this structure:

Hace + expression of time + que + verb in preterite

For example:

'Hace cinco años que me rompí la pierna' – five years ago I broke my leg.

When the preterite and imperfect are used together

The imperfect and preterite are often used together when telling a story. The imperfect provides the background, while the preterite describes the event. For example:

'Yo caminaba por el parque cuando oí un grito' – I was walking in the park when I heard a scream.

'Soñaba de los vacaciones cuando sus amigos llegaron' – He was dreaming of his holiday when his friends arrived.

When is it preterite and when is it imperfect?

Deciding whether a verb should be in preterite or imperfect normally gives English speakers huge headaches. It is not as difficult as you think though. Follow these rules to get it right:

Use the preterite to describe:

A single event that happened in the past: For example:

'Julia nació en Alemania' – Julia was born in Germany.

'Él llegó tarde a la reunión' – he arrived late to the meeting.

'Estuvimos en Londres la semana pasada' – we were in London last week.

Use the imperfect to describe something that happened:

Repeatedly in the past: 'Antes escuchaba la radio, pero ahora navego por Internet' – I used to listen to the radio but now I surf the Internet.

Age: 'Ella tenía veintidós años cuando se graduó' – she was twenty-two when she graduated.

Actions in the past which are still true: 'El supermercado tenía bolsas verdes' – the supermarket had green bags (and it still does).

Time in past: 'Era las diez de la noche cuando empezamos a comer' – it was 10 o'clock when we started to eat.

To express a characteristic of someone or something that they had throughout their existence ('era'): 'Era una casa grande pero mis abuelos eran pobres todavía' – it was a big house but my grandparents were still poor.

With 'mientras' ('while') to express two things happening at once: 'Raquel preparaba la comida mientras yo invitaba a los invitados' – Raquel prepared the food while I invited the guests.

For thinking verbs such as creer, conocer, saber and parecer: 'No sabía que tienes una hermana' – I didn't know that you had a sister.

Verbs that change meaning in the preterit and imperfect

There are some verbs that change meaning depending on whether you use preterite or imperfect. An example of this is 'conocer,' which is 'met' in preterite and 'knew' in imperfect. For example:

'Conocí un empresario el sábado' – I met an entreprenur on Saturday.
'Conocía a muchos empresarios cuando era joven' – I knew many entreprenurs when I was young. Other examples include:

	Imperfect	Preterit
Conocer	knew someone	met someone
Poder	was able to	managed to do something
No poder	wasn't be able to	failed to do something
Querer	wanted	tried to something (and failed)
No querer	didn't want	refused to do something
Tener	had	received something
Saber	knew something	found out something

14. Between the past and present: The perfect tense

In English, the present perfect expresses an action in the past that continues to now. For example:
'I have eaten strawberries and a banana today.' Or
'She has not finished her dinner so she can't watch TV'.
This is a very popular tense in Spanish and one of the easiest pasts to master and so I certainly recommend taking the time to learn it.
The present perfect is made from the verb **haber + the verb participle.**
The participle is made from dropping the verb ending and adding:
–ado for -ar verbs, such as, 'hablado' ('spoken'), 'arreglado' ('arranged') or 'terminado' ('finished').
And
–ido for -er and -ir verbs – such as, 'comido' ('eaten'), 'bebido' ('drunk'), 'elegido' ('chosen').

'Haber' changes form depending on the subject and breaks down like this:

Yo	he	nosotros/nosotras	hemos
Tú	has	nosotros/vosotras	habéis
él, ella, ud	ha	ellos, ellas, uds	han

Regular -ar, -er and –ir verbs are therefore conjugated like this:

Jugar (to play)	
he jugado	hemos jugado
has jugado	habéis jugado
ha jugado	han jugado

Correr (to run)	
he corrido	hemos corrido

| has corrido | habéis corrido |
| ha corrido | han corrido |

Subir (to go up)	
he subido	hemos subido
has subido	habéis subido
ha subido	han subido

Irregular participles

The participles of some verbs are irregular but they all end in 'o'.
These include:

abrir	Abierto
cubrir	cubierto
decir	Dicho
hacer	Hecho
disolverse	disuelto
escribir	Escrito
imprimir	impreso
morir	muerto
poner	puesto
resolver	resuelto
romper	roto
ver	visto
volver	vuelto

When is the present perfect used?

The present perfect in both English and Spanish expresses:

Something that started in the past and continues until now:

'Él ha sacado la basura hoy' – he has taken out the rubbish today.

'Hemos hablado con el jefe esta semana' – we have spoken with the boss this week.

Something that happened in the past but you don't know when or it is not important when:

'He visto todas las películas de Rocky' – I have seen all the Rocky films.

'Han visitado Nueva York – they have visited New York.

Negatives and questions

To make the above example negative you would add 'nunca' either before or after the verb or at the end of the sentence.

'Nunca he visto las películas de Rocky' – I have never seen the Rocky films.

'No han visitado Nueva York nunca' – they have never visited New York.

To make the Spanish equivalent of 'Have you ever…?' tag 'alguna vez' on the end of the question. For example:

'¿Has visto las películas de Rocky alguna vez?' – Have you ever seen the Rocky films? (Or literally, 'have you seen the Rocky films one time?')

¿Han visitado Nueva York alguna vez? – Have you ever visited New York?

> **[Spanish/English difference] The present perfect and recent time**
>
> There are, however, some important differences in the way the tense is used between the two languages. These are:
>
> In Spanish the present perfect is used to express something that has happened recently, even if the action is finished. In English, this would be said in simple past.
>
> For example:
>
> '¿Qué me has dicho?' – what did you say to me? (Or literally, 'what have you said to me?').
>
> 'Hemos comido tostadas y cereales de desayuno hoy' – we ate toast and cereal for breakfast today.

'¿Quién ha tirado la chaqueta al suelo?' – who threw the jacket on the floor?
'He sido yo' –it was me (or literally, 'I have been me').

[Spanish/English difference II] The present perfect versus the present

In English the present perfect expresses duration if the action continues to the present. For example:
'We have lived in the city for five years' or 'we have known each other since school.'
In Spanish it is more common to say this in present. The above examples would be:
'Vivimos en la ciudad desde hace cinco años' or 'hace cinco años nos conocemos.'
You can still use present perfect for duration but you must put 'durante' to express 'for.' For example:
'Hemos estudiado español durante tres años' – We have studied Spanish for three years.
'Han jugado a tenis durante seis meses' – they have played tennis for six months.

Just

Just for recent time is expressed with the verb **acabar + de + infinitive** and not the present perfect. For example:
'Acaban de llegar' – they have just arrived
'Acabamos de terminar toda la comida de la nevera' – we have just finished all the food in the fridge.

The past perfect – there was

This brings us to 'there was' + noun. 'Haber' has two possibilities in past:

'Hubo' in preterite, which runs:

Hube, hubiste, hubo, hubimos, hubisteis, hubieron + noun.

Or

'Había' in imperfect, which runs:

Había, habías, había, habíamos, habíais, habían + noun.

'Hubo' expresses a singular event in the past that is finished.
 For example:
'Hubo una tormenta la semana pasada' – there was a storm last night.

'Había' expresses something that was ongoing or <u>still exists</u>. For example:
'Había tres puertas rojas en el teatro' – there were three red doors in the theatre (and there still are).
For this reason 'hubo' is hardly used. Many Spanish speakers don't even use it when the event was singular and in the past, preferring instead 'había'.
For example, it is common to hear:
'Había una fiesta en mi barrio anoche' – there was a party in my neighbourhood last night.
'Había una reunión en el colegio de mi hermana la semana pasada' – there was a meeting at my sister's school last week.
Therefore I recommend not worrying about 'hubo' and expressing 'there was' with 'había,' as this is the way most people speak. The full structure of **había + participle** is:

Salir (to leave)	
había salido	habíamos salido
habías salido	habíais salido
había salido	habían salido

15. The continuous tense

The continuous tense expresses an action happening in the present moment. In English it is formed with 'to be' verb + gerund ('ing'). such as, 'I am walking to work.'

Spanish the present continuous is formed with **'estar'** + **verb** + **gerund**. The gerund formed by taking away the ending and adding 'ando' for '–ar' verbs and 'iendo' for -er and –ir verbs. For example:

'Estoy lavando la ropa' – I am washing the clothes.

'Está aprendiendo español' – he is learning Spanish.

'Estamos abriendo la puerta' – we are opening the door.

Irregular verbs

'Ir' and 'poder' are completely irregular.

Ir – yendo.

Poder – pudiendo.

When is the present continuous used in Spanish?

The continuous tense is ubiquitous in English and now you know the form, you may be tempted to use it all the time – however, it is not nearly so commonly used in Spanish.

The continuous is used to express:

An action that is happening right now:

'El niño está durmiendo en la cama – the child is sleeping in the bed.'

'Estoy preparando la cena' – I am preparing dinner.

An action that is ongoing (though may not be happening at this moment):

'Él está aprendiendo francés' – he is learning French.

With the adverb mientras (while) to express two ongoing actions:

'Él estaba limpiando la casa mientras ella estaba regando las plantas' – he was cleaning the house while she was watering the plants.

With llevar + verb in gerund to express an action that started in the past and continues into the present:

'Llevan dos años trabajando aquí' – they have been working here for two years.
'Llevo cantando profesionalmente desde hace tres años – I have been singing professionally for three years.

[Spanish/English Difference] When the continuous is not used in Spanish

The continuous is not used:

For the future: This is normally expressed in present or future tense.
'Estudiaré todo el fin de semana' – I am studing all weekend.
'Vuelo a Paris el viernes' – I am flying to Paris on Friday.

Exclamations: This is also normally expressed in present tense.
'¡Qué haces!' – What are you doing!
'¿Por qué no juegas con nosotros?' – Why aren't you playing with us?

At the beginning of sentences: This is always with the infinitive of the verb.
'Bailar es bueno para la alma' – dancing is good for the soul.
'Cocinar fuera es más divertido – cooking outside is more fun.

After prepositions: This is also always the infinitive.
'Juan tiene miedo de dormir solo' – Juan is scared of sleeping alone.

In addition to these rules, remember that while English speakers tend to lean towards speaking in continuous, Spanish speakers lean towards the present simple. Therefore many sentences where you would use continuous in English you would often put into present in Spanish, particularly about things that are not happening at this minute. For example:
'Intento no gastar tanto dinero este mes' – I am trying not to spend so much money this month.

'Me hace ilusión conocer a tu hermano' – I am looking forward to meeting your brother.
'Me encuentro mal, me voy a casa' – I am feeling sick, I am going home.

Uses in past

You can also change to past with estaba (imperfect) or estuvo (preterite). The same rules apply; if the action is finished, use the preterite. However, if the action happened over a long period of time, or continues to be true, use the imperfect. For example:
'Los niños estuvieron estudiando inglés ayer' – the children were studying English yesterday.
'Estaba pensando en abandonar mis estudios' – I was thinking about dropping out of college (and I am still thinking about it).

Verbs used with continuous

Verbs such as **'seguir'** and **'continuar'** are often followed by a verb in continuous as they emphasise that an action continues. 'Seguir' can be thought of as the verb 'to keep' or the adverb 'still' in English. For example:
'Sigue trabajando en el colegio' –she is still working at the school
'Siguen jugando a videojuegos y no estudiando' – they keep playing video games and not studying.
'Ella continuó durmiendo mientras sonaba el teléfono' – she continued sleeping while the telephone rang.
Motion verbs such as **'andar'** and **'ir'** are also often followed by a verb in continuous to express the action. In addition, **ir + movement verb** in continuous expresses the 'mode of movement'. For example:
'Vamos corriendo al colegio cada mañana' – we run to school every morning (or literally 'we go running to school…')
'Ve caminando durante cinco minutos en esa direción y verás el monestario' – walk for five minutes and you will see the monestry.

16. Reflexives

Reflexives consist of the **verb + a reflexive pronoun**. They express that the subject does the action to themselves. For example:

'Ella se cortó con el cuchillo' – she cut herself with the knife.

'Él canta cuando se ducha – he sings to himself when he takes a shower (or in Spanish, 'showers himself).

Spanish reflexive pronouns are:

me	myself
te	yourself
se	yourself (formal), himself, herself
nos	ourselves
os	yourselves
se	themselves

For example:

Despertarse (to wake up)	
me despierto	nos despertamos
te despiertas	os despertáis
se despierta	se despiertan

Placement of the reflexive

If there is only one verb in the sentence the reflexive usually goes before the verb as a stand-alone word.

'Me despierto a las siete por la mañana' – I wake up at seven o'clock in the morning.

If there are two or more verbs in the sentence the reflexive goes either before the verb as a stand-alone word or at the end, joined to last verb.

'Se va a lavar' or 'va a lavarse' – he is going to wash himself.

If you have two reflexive verbs together (referring to the same subject), then only use one reflexive. For example:

'Quiere afeitar y peinarse' – he wants to wash and comb himself.

When do you use the reflexive?

Spanish uses reflexives far more than English and you are probably wondering why. Take a look at the cases below.

Case 1: Personal care

Personal grooming is something you do to yourself, these verbs are therefore reflexive. In Spanish you wouldn't say 'I am going to have a bath' but rather 'I am going to bath myself' ('voy a bañarme'). Equally you don't say 'to get dressed' but rather 'to dress yourself'.

Take a look at these personal care verbs below.

Afeitarse – to shavelavarse to wash

Abrigarse – to put on a coat

Bañarse – to bath

Cepillarse – to brush

Ducharse – to shower

Limarse – to file ones nails

Mirarse – to look at oneself

Maquillarse – to put on makeup

Peinarse – to comb ones hair

Pintarse (los labios) – to put on lipstick

Ponerse – to put on (clothes)

Quitarse – to take off

Secarse – to dry oneself

Vestirse – to get dressed

Other common reflexive verbs

These verbs have no common category, however, they are all reflexive.

Acordarse de – to remember.
Acostarse – to go to bed.
Despedirse – to say to goodbye.
Divertirse – to have fun.
Dormirse – to fall asleep.
Llamarse – to call someone a name.
Olvidarse de – to forget.
Probarse – to try (something).
Sentarse – to sit.
Sentirse – to feel.

Case 2: When the reflexive is 'get' in English

You may be wondering how to say, 'I got lost' or 'I am getting cold'? Well, in Spanish this is often expressed with the reflexive verb meaning that instead of saying something happened to you, you say you did it to yourself. The above examples would be:

'Me perdí' (literally, 'I lost myself') and 'me estoy enfriando' ('I am cooling myself').

More 'get' reflexives

Aburrirse de – to get bored of.
Acercarse a– to get close to.
Calentarse – to get hot.
Cansarse – to get tired.
Casarse con – to get married to.
Confundirse – to get confused.
Disgustarse de/con – to get upset by or with.
Divorciarse – to get divorced.
Descontrolarse – go out of control.
Drogarse – to get high.
Emocionarse – to get excited.

Emborracharse – to get drunk.

Enfadarse con – to get angry with.

Enfermarse – to get sick.

Enfriarse – to get cold.

Estinguirse – to become extinct.

Estresarse por – to get stressed about.

Marearse – to get dizzy.

Mojarse – to get wet.

Oscurecerse – to get dark.

Perderse – to get lost.

Preocuparse – to get worried.

Prepararse – to get ready/prepared.

Quemarse – to get burnt.

Case 3: When the reflexive means the general 'you'
In English 'you' can mean 'you' singular, plural or the general 'you' expressed in the past as 'one'. For example:
'You can't live on Mars yet' – this is not referring to an individual but rather everybody.
In Spanish this is made with **se + verb in third person singular** or **plural.** It is most commonly used with the verb 'poder' (to be able to). For example:
'No se puede esquiar en verano' – you (or one) can't ski in summer.
'Se pagan los impuestos a fin del año – you pay your taxes at the end of the year.
'Se puede vivir sin coche' – one can live without a car.

Case 4: Emphasis
The reflexive is used for emphasis. In English this would often be expressed with the preposition 'up'. For example:
'Se lo comió todo' – he ate it all up.
'¡Estúdiatelo!' – really study it!

Strengthening the reflexive

Sometimes you want to emphasis that you and no other did or made something.

For example:

'She made that cake *herself*.'

In Spanish this would be 'ella se hizo la tarta a sí misma.'

These are called reflexive pronouns and they go at the end of the sentence to emphasise who did the action. They change ending depending on the gender of the person.

A mí mismo/a – myself.

A ti mismo/a – yourself.

A sí mismo/a – himself, herself.

A nosotros/as mismos/as – ourselves.

A vosotros/as mismos/as – yourselves.

A sí mismos/as – themselves.

Each other

While reflexives mean the interaction with the self, each other means an interaction with another. In Spanish 'each other' is also expressed in reflexive with either 'se' or 'nos.' For example:

'Nos conocemos desde hace mucho tiempo' – we have known each other a long time ago.

'Se quieren mucho' – they love each other a lot.

'Nos vemos el lunes y hablamos más del asunto' – we will see each other on Monday and speak with each other more about the subject.

'Se parecen, tus hijos' – your children look like each other.

The other way to say 'each other' is by using **el uno al otro** for masculine or neutral subjects and **la una a la otra** for feminine. This form adds clarification and emphasis but it is still be placed with the verb in reflexive. For example:

'Ayer, jugaban el uno con el otro en el jardín' – they were playing with each other yesterday in the garden.

'Se dieron un regalo el uno al otro' – they gave each other a present.

'Nos vemos, la una a la otra, como amigas' – we see each other as friends.

Verbs that change meaning with reflexive

There are many verbs that use the reflexive to change their meaning and so it is important to remember when to use it or the listener might get completely the wrong idea. Take a look at the sentences below.

Abonar – to pay / **Abonarse** – to subscribe to a publication or buy a season ticket.

Acordar – to agree / **Acordarse** – to remember.

Acusar – to accuse someone of something / **Acusarse** – to admit something.

'Me acuso de ser drogadicto' – I admitted to being a drug addict.

Animar – to encourage to do something / **Animarse** – to feel like doing something.

'Vamos al cine, ¿te animas? – we are going to the cinema, do you feel like it?

Aparecer – to appear / **Aparecerse** – to appear with a supernatural event.

Abrir – to open / **Abrirse** – to open up/to confide.

Cerrar – to close / **Cerrarse** – to close yourself off.

Combinar – to combine or to match / **Combinarse** – to take turns.

Cambiar – to change / **Cambiarse** – to switch.

'Nos cambiamos a Telefónica' – We switched to Telefonica.

Dormir – to sleep / **Dormirse** – To fall asleep.

'Se duermió una noche escuchando la radio' – she fell asleep one night listening to the radio.

Gastar – to spend / **Gastarse** – to run down or to wear out.

Ir – to go / **Irse** – to leave.

Llevar – to carry something / **Llevarse** – to steal something.

Morir –to die accidentally / **Morirse** – to die naturally.

Encontrar – to find/meet someone / **Encontrarse** – to find somebody by chance.

Negar – deny / **Negarse** – to refuse a request.

Olvidar – to forget intentionally / **Olvidarse** – to forget accidentally.

Ocurrir – to occur / **Ocurrirse** – to suddenly have an idea.

Pelar – to peel / **Pelarse** – to shave your head.

Poner – to put / **Ponerse** – to put on clothes.

Reír – to laugh / **Reírse** – to laugh at.

Salir – to leave/ **Salirse** – to leave unexpectedly/to leak.

Saltar – to jump / **Saltarse** –to jump over, skip an event or avoid obligation.

'Más chinos se saltan la ley del hijo unico' – More Chinese people avoid the only child law.

Volver – to return / **Volverse** – turn around or make an unexpected return.

17. The subjunctive in present

In Spanish there are two ways of speaking; one is <u>indicative</u> where the speaker talks about actions or events which they are certain are true. This is expressed in all normal tenses – the present, the past, continuous and so on. The second way is <u>subjunctive</u> when the speaker is not certain about an action or event, most likely because they are not the person who will do the action.

Think of it like this: we are both going to a party and when you arrive I want you to call me. I know for sure when I will arrive as I am in control of this action, but I am not sure when you will arrive and so I say:

'Cuándo lleg<u>ues</u> a la fiesta llámame' (in subjunctive form) as opposed to 'cuándo lleg<u>as</u> a la fiesta llámame' (in indicative).

This I am sure throws up lots of questions about when exactly the speaker has sufficient doubt to use the subjunctive. But don't worry, the subjunctive is not an arbitrary tense that people use if and when they feel like it. There are strict rules about when to use it, all of which I will go into. But first let's look at the structure.

If the verb ends in an -ar in infinitive, you change the 'a' to 'e'. Likewise, if it ends in an -er or -ir you change it to 'a'. The 'o' of the 'yo' form completely disappears. Take a look at these tables:

Arreglar	**Entender**	**Escribir**
arregle	entienda	escribe
arregles	entiendas	escribes
arregle	entienda	escribe
arreglemos	entendamos	escribamos
arregléis	entendáis	escribáis
arreglen	entiendan	escriban

<u>NOTE:</u> The first and third person forms have the same endings.

<u>NOTE:</u> Also that stem changing verbs such as entender keep their form but with a different ending. More examples:

Verb	Indicative	Subjunctive
pensar	piensa	piense
perder	pierde	pierda
escoger	escoje	escoja
dormir	duerme	duerma
incluir	incluye	incluya

Irregular verbs in 'yo' form

Verbs that are irregular in the 'yo' form that end with 'go' change to 'ga' for all persons of the verb in subjunctive. For example:

Caer: Caiga, caigas, caiga, caigamos, caigáis, caigan.
Hacer: Haga, hagas, haga, hagamos, hagáis, hagan.
Poner: Ponga, pongas, ponga, pongamos, pongáis, pongan.
Salir: Salga, salgas, salgamos, salgáis, salgan.
Traer: Traiga, traigas, traiga, traigamos, traigáis, traigan.
Valer: Valga, valgas, valga, valgamos, valgáis, valgan.

Other irregular verbs in the present

Dar	dé, des, dé, demos, deis, den
Estar	esté, estés, esté, estemos, estéis, estén
Haber	haya, hayas, hayas, hayamos, hayáis, hayan
Ir	vaya, vayas, vaya, vayamos, vayáis, vayan
Saber	sepa, sepas, sepa, sepamos, sepáis, sepan
Ser	sea, seas, sea, seamos, seáis, sean
Caber	quepa, quepas, quepa, quepamos, quepáis, quepan
Ver	vea, veas, vea, veamos, veáis, vean

When do you use the subjunctive?

The short the answer is after 'que,' but let's give some more clarification. Imagine you need to ask your friend to do something. In English this would be with the verb 'want' or 'need' + infinitive. For example:

'I want you to buy some bread at the supermarket.'

Spanish doesn't work like this; between 'want' and 'buy' there is a **que + subjunctive** meaning that the sentence runs:

'I want that you buy some bread at the supermarket' or 'Quiero que compres pan en el supermecardo.'

The 'que' + subjunctive adds doubt, making it more polite; I know if I will go to the supermarket but I don't know if you will go for me. If you're speaking about yourself, you know what you will do and so the structure is 'querer + infinitive':

'Quiero comprar pan en el supermercardo...' – I want to buy bread in the supermarket...

'Pero quiero que vayas a la papelaría' – but I want you to go to the stationery shop.

Verbs with que + subjunctive when speaking about what someone else will do and + infinitive when speaking about what you will do.

Aconsejar que – to advise that.

Te aconsejo que comas mejor – I advise you to eat more (or I advise that you eat better)

Dejar que – to allow that.

Decidir que – to decide.

Conseguir – to manage/to achieve.

Esperar que – to hope that.

Exigir que – to demand that.

Insistir que – to insist that.

Impedir que – to stop that.

Mandar que – to order that.

Necesitar que – to need that.

Pedir que – to ask that.
Pensar que – to think that.
Permitir que – to permit that.
Preferir que – to prefer that.
Prohibir que – to prohibit.
Proponer que – to propose that.
Recomendar que – to recommend that.
Recordar que – to remember that.
Rogar que – to beg that.
Sugerir que – to suggest that.

Phrases with que + subjunctive

In addition many 'ser' + adjective phrases expressing opinion are also used with que + subjunctive as again you are not talking about what you will do but rather what will happen to someone or something else.

Es aconsejable que – it's advisable that.
Es bueno que – it's good that.
Es fantástico que – it's fantastic that.
Es importante que – it's important that.
Es imposible que – it's impossible that.
Es incierto que – it's uncertain that.
Es increíble que – it's incredible that.
Es una lástima que – it's a shame that.
Es malo que – it's bad that.
Es mejor que – it's better that.
Es necesario que – it's necessary that.
Es raro que – it's weird that.
Es ridículo que – it's ridiculous that.
Es terrible que – it's terrible that.

Opinions

Opinion verbs such as:

'Creer que', 'opinar que', 'pensar que', 'parecer que', 'estar de acuerdo con lo que' are expressed in indicative in positive but subjunctive in negative.

For example:

'Creo que él trabaja los sábados...' – I think he works on Saturdays...

'Pero no creo que trabaje los domingos...' – but I don't think he works on Sundays.

'Me parece que hace buen trabajo' –....it seems to me that he does good work.

'pero no me pareca que le guste...' – but it doesn't seem to me that he likes it.

Opinions II: Parecer in subjunctive and indicative

Parecer means 'to seem' in English, so when you use it in an opinion sentence you're saying 'It seems to me that...'

Affirmative sentences run:

Indirect object pronoun + parece que + indicative

'Me parece que Patricia es muy simpática' – it seems to me that Patricia is very kind.

While negative sentences run:

Indirect object pronoun + parece que + subjunctive

'No le parece que Patricia sea simpática' – it doesn't seem to him that Patricia is kind.

Things change, however, when you add an adjective between 'parecer' and 'que' to express your opinions about someone or something.

In this case it is:

Indirect object pronoun + parece + adjective + que + subjunctive

'Me parece increíble que algunas personas no reciclen' – It seems to be incredible that some people don't recycle.

'Me parece mejor que vayas a Barcelona' – It seems to me better that you go to Barcelona.

If your opinion is general there is no 'que' and the following verb is in infinitive.

'Me parece interesante estudiar medicina' – I think studying medicine is interesting.

'Les parece bueno correr por la mañana' – they think it's good to run in the morning.

Phrases with probability

'May' and 'might' are expressed in many ways in Spanish, most of which are followed by the subjunctive to emphasise the doubt. Here are some options.

Posiblemente/probablemente + subjunctive

Puede que + subjunctive

'Puede que haya un solución' – there could be a solution.

Puede ser que – it could be that.

Es posible que –it's possible that.

Es probable que – it's likely that.

Es improbable que –it's unlikely that.

Es dudoso que –it's doubtful that.

Imperative in negative

We use the imperative when we want to give someone a command. We do this in English by omitting the subject (I, you, he, she etc) to make sentences such as 'close the door', 'open your books' and 'look at me.'

In Spanish, commands are made with the verb in third person singular or plural in indicative. The above sentences would be in singular form:

'Cierra la puerta', 'Abre los libros' and 'Mírame'

And in plural form:

'Cerrad la puerta', 'abrid los libros' and 'miradme'

In negative, however, the verb is in subjunctive. For example:

'Ponme patatas pero no me pongas col' – give me (or literally put me) potatoes but don't give me cabbage.'

'Toca la cámara si deseas pero no toques la pintura' – touch the camera if you wish but don't touch the painting.'

'Me voy y no me busquéis' – I am leaving and don't search for me.

Negatives phrases + subjunctive

Phrases in negative are by definition doubtful, so are in subjunctive when you are talking about another's actions that aren't proven. When speaking about another's actions that are proven use indicative. For example:

'¿El motivo por el que no has aprobado los exámenes no es porque no estudies?' – The reason why you haven't passed your exams isn't because you don't study?

In this statement there are two actions, one of which is proven (the person hasn't passed their exams) and one which is not proven (that they don't study). It is this action that is in subjunctive.

Again, when you are talking about your own actions it is with indicative.

More examples:

No es que + subjunctive

'¿No es que no quieras venir al concierto conmigo?' – it isn't because you don't want to come to the concert with me?

'No, no es que no quiera ir contingo, es que tengo otras cosas que hacer' – no, it isn't because I don't want to go with you, it's because I have other things to do.

No es porque + subjunctive
No puede ser que + subjunctive

'¿El motivo por el retraso no puede ser que esté malito?' – the reason for his lateness couldn't be because he is sick?

So that – para que

While 'para' + infinitive means 'in order to', 'para que' means 'so that,' which always carries an element of doubt and is in subjunctive. For example:

'Lleva la camisa azul para que te reconozca' – wear the blue shirt so that I recognise you.

'Te presto mi bici para que tus hijos aprendan a montarla' – I will lend you my bike so that your children learn to ride it.

Some verbs are normally only followed by 'para que' + verb in subjunctive.

These are:

Convencerse para que – to convince

'Le intentaré convencer de ir contigo para que tengas un compañero' – I will try to convince him to go with you do so that you will have a companion.

Informarse para que – to inform

'Les informaré para que sepan dónde es la boda' – I'll inform them so that they know where the wedding is.

Persuadir para que – to pursade

'Intenta persuadirles para que podamos tomar prestado su coche' – try to pursade them to lend us the car.

Cuando + subjunctive and indicative

Verbs following cuándo can be in both subjunctive or indicative depending on the situation.

If you are referring to events in past or if it is something you do as a routine it is **cuando + indicative**. For example:

'Cuando voy a la piscina suelo ver a mis amigos' – when I go to the swimming pool I usually see my friends.

'Cuando le vi en el parque llevaba puesta una gorra' – when I saw him in the park he was wearing a cap.

If cuando refers to the future or present for an action that doesn't habitually happen it is **cuando + subjunctive.** For example:

'Cuando vayamos a París comeremos caracoles' – when we go to Paris we will eat snails.

'Cuando lleguéis a casa llamadme' – when you lot arrive home, call me.

In this way the cuando + subjunctive usually refers to an action that someone else will do alone or with you, so you don't have total control over when it might happen.

Another way to use cuando + subjunctive is to be polite. For example, your friend may invite you to dinner and ask what time you will meet and you answer:

'Cuando quieras' – when you want (or a better translation would be 'when you wish').

Hay + Subjunctive

If 'hay' is used with 'alguien', 'algo', or 'algún', 'alguno', 'alguna' the structure runs:

Hay + alguien + que + subjunctive. For example:

'¿Hay alguien que hable inglés?' – is there anyone who speaks English?

'¿Hay algo que pueda comer en la nevera?' – is there anything that I can eat in the fridge?

'¿Hay algún sitio por aquí donde vendan cerámica?' – is there some place around here where they sell ceramics?

No hay + subjunctive

If the sentence is negative then the structure runs:

No hay nadie, nada, ningún, ninguno/a + noun + subjunctive.

For example:

'No hay ningún hotel donde pueda dormir esta noche – there is no hotel where we can sleep tonight (or there isn't any hotel where we can sleep tonight).
'No hay nadie que me ayude' – there isn't anyone who can help me or there is no one who can help me.
'No hay nada que le detenga' – there isn't anything to stop him or There is nothing to stop him.

Conocer que in indicative and subjunctive

When speaking about someone or somewhere you know exists, use **conocer (+ que) + indicative.**

When speaking about someone/somewhere that you are not sure exists use **conocer + que + subjunctive.** For this reason the subjunctive form is most commonly used in questions. For example:

'¿Conoces a alguien que se llame Antonio?' – do you know anyone called Antonio?

'¿Conocen un restaurant que tenga un menú del día?' – do they know a restaurant that has a menu of the day?

'Conozco una chica que habla seis idiomas perfectamente' – I know a girl who can speak six languages perfectly.'

Buscar que in indicative and subjunctive

When you know what you are looking for exists use **'buscar' + indicative** and when you don't know it exists use **buscar + que + subjunctive**. For example:

'Busco un profesor que viva cerca de mi casa' – I am looking for a teacher that lives near my house.

'Busco un hotel por Internet que tiene piscina' – I am looking for a hotel (that I know) online that has a swimming pool.

'Busco un hotel por Internet que tenga piscina' – I am looking for a hotel (that may or may not exist) online that has a swimming pool.

Before, after and until in subjunctive and indicative

The normal antes de (before) and después de (after) and hasta (until) are used with indicative. However, when speaking about an action and you're not sure when it will happen, you add 'que' plus sunjunctive. For example:

Antes de que + subjunctive – before that

'Vuelve a casa antes de que empieze a llover' – come back home before it rains.

Después de que + subjunctive – after that

'Después de que reciba la carta, le llamarán' – after receiving the letter they will call her.

Hasta que + until that

'Hasta que sepa la verdad sigue como siempre' – until he knows the truth, carry on as usual.

Phrases + subjunctive

Here are some common phrases expressed with subjunctive.

Por si acaso + subjunctive – just in case.

'Toma el paraguas por si acaso llueve' – take the umbrella just in case it rains.

'Qué yo sepa + indicative ('sepa' is the subjunctive of 'saber') – as far as I know

'Qué yo sepa ya han almorzado – as far as I know they have already eaten.

'En cuanto + subjunctive – as soon as.

'Llámanos en cuanto tengas tiempo' – call us as soon as you have time.

Siempre y cuando + subjunctive – as long as.

'Limpiaré la casa siempre y cuando hagas la compra' – I will clean the house as long as you do the shopping.

Con tal de que + subjunctive – provided that.

'Te presto el coche con tal de que tengas cuidado' – I will lend you the car provided that you take care.

A condicion de que + subjunctive – on condition that.

'Te llevo al medico a condición de que sigas su consejo' – I will take you to the doctor on condition that you follow their advice.

Commands and exclamations

Que + subjunctive has no direct translation in English. It expresses a desire or hope. If you are sick a friend may say 'que te mejores pronto' meaning 'I hope you get better soon'. It is very common and worth studying if you want to sound like a native. More examples

Que os divirtáis – I hope you enjoy yourself/ may you enjoy yourself.

Que descanse en paz – let him rest in peace.

Que sea pronto – I hope it's soon.

Que no me vean así – don't let them see me like this.

The present perfect subjunctive

The present perfect subjunctive is **'haber' (in subjunctive) + participle**. It is conjugated like this:

Haber comido (to have eaten)
haya comido
hayas comido
haya comido
hayamos comido
hayáis comido
hayan comido

It is used after certain verbs, adjectives or interrogatives + 'que' under the same conditions as the present subjunctive. For example:

'Cuando hayan acabado con el informe, pueden empezar con la presentación' – when they have finished with the report they can start with the presentation.

'¿Hay alguien aquí que haya estado en Milán?' – is there anyone here who has been to Milan?

'Me parece tonto que hayan cambiado los monumentos tanto' – it seems to me crazy that they have changed the monuments so much.

Finally phrases that are always + indicative

Phrases that make an evaluation keep the indicative. For example:

'Es lógico que saque buenas notas, es inteligente' – it's logical that he gets good marks, he is intelligent. More examples:

Es lógico que – it's logical that.

Es normal que – it's normal that.

Es una pena que – it's a shame that.

Es malo que – it's bad that.

Es fundamental que – it's fundermental that.

Es vergonzoso que – it's shameful that.

Es injusto que + indicativo –it's not fair that.

Seguro que + indicativo – for sure.

Me parece que + indicative – it seems that/ it looks like.

Me imagino que + indicative – I guess that..

Es obvio que – it is obvious that.

Es verdad que – it's true that.

No hay duda que – there is no doubt that.

No dudar que – to not doubt that.

Estar seguro que – to be sure that.

18. The past subjunctive and if clauses

If clauses

The past subjunctive is something called the second conditional in English. A typical sentence runs like this:

'If I had a yacht, I would sail around the world.' The verb after 'if' is in simple past (had), but you are not speaking about the past. Instead you are referring to now, about something you don't have.

We change have to had in this case to show the listener that are speaking about something that isn't currently real. Spanish has the same idea but instead of changing a present verb to past it changes it to the past subjunctive; a different tense entirely. The above sentence would therefore be:

'Si tuviera un yate, navegaría por el mundo.'

The second half of the sentence contains 'would sail'. Would is made in Spanish with the conditional tense (by adding an -ía conjugation to the end of the verb). For more information see The Conditionals chapter.

Before we speak more about the uses of the past subjunctive let's look at how to conjugate it.

Ar verbs

The past subjunctive is formed by putting the verb in the preterite third person singular, then taking off the 'ó' and adding appropriate conjugation. For example:

'Hablar' becomes 'habló' in preterite third person singular, 'comprar' becomes 'compró', 'llevar' becomes 'llevó'.

To make them past subjunctive conjugate like this.

Hablar	Comprar	Llevar
hablara	comprara	llevara
hablaras	comparas	llevaras

hablara	comprara	llevara
habláramos	compráramos	lleváramos
hablarais	comprarais	llevarais
hablaran	compraran	llevaran

Alarm bells may now be ringing as this conjugation looks very similar to future. So how do you distinguish between the two?

Well the answer is that future conjugations carry an accent (except nosotros form), so end with a harder á sound. This conjugation carries no accents (except nosotros, which does) and so has a soft ending.

Er and ir verbs

To conjugate these verbs again change the verb to preterite, third person singular. Take away the 'ó' and add the appropriate ending.

Poder becomes 'pudo' in preterite third person singular, 'tener' becomes 'tuvo', 'venir' 'vino' and 'decidir' 'decidió'.

To make them past subjunctive conjugate like this.

Poder	**Tener**	**Venir**	**Decedir**
Pudiera	tuviera	viniera	decidiera
Pudieras	tuvieras	vineiras	decidieras
Pudiera	tuviera	viniera	decidiera
pudiéramos	tuviéramos	viniéramos	decidiéramos
Pudierais	tuvierais	vinierais	deciderais
Pudieran	tuverian	vinieran	decideran

Irregular verbs in preterite third person

If the verb is irregular in preterite then it naturally becomes irregular in the past subjunctive. Take a look at these irregular verbs.

Verb	Preterite	Past subjunctive
andar	anduvo	anduviera
caber	cupo	cupiera
caer	cayó	cayera
dar	dio	diera
decir	dijo	dijera
ser and ir	fue	fuera
poner	puso	pusiera
poder	pudo	pudiera
ver	vio	viera
querer	quiso	quisiera

The second way to make the past subjunctive

There is another conjugation for the past subjunctive and that is again to change the verb to third person, singular, preterite and add 'ase' for -ar verbs and 'ese' for -er and -ir verbs. For example:

Aterrizar (To land)	Pedir (to ask for)	Caer (to fall)
aterrase	pidiese	cayese
aterrases	pidieses	cayeses
aterrase	pidiese	cayese
aterrásemos	pidiésemos	cayésemos
aterraseis	pidieseis	cayeseis
aterrasen	pidiesen	cayesen

It is not as commonly used as the 'ara' or 'iesa' and so from now on I will refer to the first form.

When is the past subjunctive used?

To understand the reason for the past subjunctive I refer you again to the first example:

'Si tuviera un yate, navegaría por el mundo' – if I had a yacht, I would sail the world.

This sentence, known as the second conditional, expresses something that is not real ('I don't have a yacht') but is still possible ('I could have a yacht if I earnt more money').

Its structure in English runs:

If + past simple + would + verb in infinitive without 'to' (which makes the conditional).

The Spanish version is exactly the same but instead of past simple you use past subjunctive.

Si + past subjunctive + verb in conditional

More examples:

'Si comieras menos chocolate, perderías peso' – if you ate less chocolate you would lose weight.

'Si él no fumara saldría con él' – if he didn't smoke, I would go out with him.

'Si quisiéramos impedir el cambio climatico dejaríamos de conducir coches' – if we wanted to stop climate change we would stop driving cars.

'Si no nos gustara España, no viviríamos aquí' – if we didn't like Spain, we wouldn't live here.

Other uses of the past subjunctive

But there is more to the past subjunctive than 'if' statements. Paired together with certain helper statements, it opens the door for a whole load of things you say in English. Take a look at these phrases:

A menos que, excepto que, salvo que, a no ser que – unless.

Siempre y cuando – as long as.

Con tal de que – provided that.

All of these phrases are + subjunctive in either present or past. In English it works the same but with either will + present (present subjunctive in Spanish) or past + would (past subjunctive). Take a look at these examples.

If something is very likely to happen the sentence runs:
Subject + future + helper phrase + subjunctive in present
Example: 'Iré al cine a menos que tenga que trabajar' – I will go to the cinema unless I have to work. More examples:
'Te compraré la chaqueta siempre y cuando la lleves' – I will buy you the jacket as long as you wear it.
'La maestra me dejará salir pronto con tal de que explique por qué al director' – the teacher will let me leave early provided that I explain why to the head.
'No iréa la fiesta a no ser que me llame' – I am not going to the party unless they call me.

If something is not currently real (but could be) the sentence runs:
Object + conditional + helper phrase + past subjunctive.
Or more commonly:
Helper phrase + object + past subjunctive + conditional.
'Siempre y cuando compráramos una tienda podríamos ir de cámping este fin de semana' – as long as we bought a tent, we could go camping this weekend.

More examples:
'Él aceptaría el trabajo con tal de que le pagasen las horas extras' – he would accept the job provided that they paid him overtime.
'Ella nunca llevaría tacones a menos que fuera para una boda' – she would never wear heels unless it was for a wedding.
'Siempre y cuando vinieras conmigo, no me quejaría' – as long as you came with me, I wouldn't complain.

Even though and Even if

'Even if' and 'even though' are sentence connectors that join two clauses that seem in opposition. For example, 'even though it is raining, we will go for a picnic.' The fact that it is raining and we will go for a picnic are two opposing ideas, and so they are connected with an 'even though.' Similar words include 'despite' and 'however'.

Even though

'Even though/although' expresses something that is real (it really is raining, we really are going for a picnic). It is therefore never placed with conditional.
Its equivalent in Spanish is **aunque + indicative.** For example:
'Aunque le gusta el fútbol, no quiere ver el partido' – even though he likes football he doesn't want to see the match.
'Antes estudiaba la ley aunque quería hacerse actor' – he used to study law even though he wanted to become an actor.

Even if

'Even if' in English expresses something that isn't – real meaning that it is paired with a conditional; either present + will, past + would or the third conditional (which I will talk about in the next chapter).
In Spanish it is **aunque + subjunctive** either in present or past.
If what you're talking about is very possible it is **present + will** in English and **+ present subjunctive** in Spanish. For example:
'Aunque no trabajemos esta semana, tenemos que ir a la conferencia el sábado' – even if we don't work this week we will still have to go to the conference on Saturday.
'Aunque no sepa el temario me presentaré al examen' – even if I don't know the syllabus I will take the exam.
If what you're talking about is very improbable use **past + would** in English and past **subjunctive + conditional** in Spanish. For example:

'Aunque tuviera más tiempo no podría ir de vacaciones' – even if I had more time, I couldn't go on holiday.

'Aunque les gustara el arte no irían al museao de arte' – even if they liked art, they wouldn't go to the art gallery.

'Te enfadarías aunque llegara a la fiesta a tiempo' – even if I arrived at the party on time, you would still be angry with me.

As if and as though

'As if' and 'as though' are conjugations used to make a metaphor or simile. They often express something negative.In Spanish this is 'ni que' or 'como si.' If what you're saying is likely to be true the structure of 'ni que/como si' is:

Subject + present + ni qué + present subjunctive

For example:

'Hablas ni que te gustase el baloncesto' – you speak as if you like basketball

'Parece como si tuviese hambre' – she looks as if she is hungry.

If what you're saying isn't true or isn't real then the structure is:
'Subject + present + ni qué/como si + past subjunctive

For example:

'Baila como si fuera una bailarina' – she dances as if she were a ballerina.

'Comes ni que estuvieras muriendo de hambre' – you eat as if you were dying of hunger.

'Gastan dinero ni que no tuvieran una deuda' – they spend money as if they didn't have a debt.

As you can probably tell from the equivalent in English, 'ni que' and 'como si' are more commonly used when speaking about something that is not real.

If I were you/si yo fuera tú

This is one of the most useful past subjunctive phrases and has a direct translation in English. Have a look at these examples below. Note that it is not the object pronoun that comes after 'fuera' (le, les and so on) but the subject pronoun.

'Si yo fuera ella no saldría con él' – if I were her I wouldn't go out with him.
'Si yo fuera ellos cambaría la fecha de la boda' – if I were them I would change the date of the wedding.

Yo de ti

Another way to say 'if I were you' is **yo de + prepositional pronoun + conditional**. For example:
'Yo de ti buscaría otro puesto' – if I were you, I would look for another position.
'Yo de él no compraría el piso' – if I were him, I wouldn't buy the flat.

Mixed conditionals

Just like English, Spanish mixes the hypothetical and real depending on the context. Take a look at these examples:
'Aunque él hiciera los deberes, ¿dónde están ahora?' – even if he did his homework, where is it now?
Here the boy may or may not have done his homework, so we use simple past in English and past subjunctive in Spanish. However, the fact you can't find the homework is real, so this is present in both cases. More examples:
'Aunque supiera la verdad, ¿por qué debería decírtela? – even if I knew the truth, why should I tell you?
'Y, aunque ella pudiera esquiar, no voy a ir a la montaña' – and even if she could ski, I am not going to the mountain.

Verbs that change their meaning with the subjunctive

There are a handful of verbs that change their meaning with the subjunctive. The most useful is 'esperar' which + indicative means 'to expect' and + subjunctive means 'to hope.' Let's look at some examples.

'Espero que vendrá al cumpleaños' – I expect you to come to the birthday party.

'Espero que vengas al cumpleaños' – I hope that you come to the birthday party.

'Esperan que sacaré buenas notas' –they expect me to get good marks.

'Esperan que saque buenas notas' – they hope I get good marks.

Note, however, that 'esperar' to mean 'expect' is usually only found in literature. Most of the time people use the verb with subjunctive to mean 'hope' and 'creer' or 'pensar' (believe and think) to say that you expect something to happen.

Esperar when you are the subject and when someone else is the subject

When the action refers to something you will do it is **esperar + infinitive**, when in refers to someone else it is **esperar + que + subjunctive**. For example:

'Espero ganar mucho dinero' – I hope to win lots of money.

'Espero que ganes mucho dinero' – I hope that you win lots of money.

Ojalá – wish or hope

Ojalá means 'to wish' or 'to hope' affirmative and negative sentences.

Its structure runs: **Ojalá + present or past subjunctive** (depending on the probability of the statement). For example:

'Ojalá que reparen el ordenador hoy' – I hope that they repair the computer today.

'Ojaolá pudiera jubilarme' – I wish I could retire.

'Ojalá no tuviera un gato' – I wish I didn't have a cat.

It is not, however, used in questions. For the interrogative you must instead use a verb such as 'querer' or 'desear.'

Hopefully is expressed with 'con suerte.' For example:

'¿A qué hora llega tu hijo?' '¡A las tres con suerte!' – what time does your son arrive. At three hopefully!

19. The pluperfect subjunctive

The final subjunctive is the pluperfect (or third conditional in English). It is used when speaking about a hypothetical past. For example:
'Si hubiera conseguido el trabajo, habría comprado un coche nuevo' – If I had got the job, I would have bought a new car.
'Si hubiera aprobado el examen, te lo habría dicho' – If I had passed the exam, I would have told you.
This entire sentence refers to something that is an impossible, alternative past.

Structure
The structure relys on 'haber' in past subjunctive and conditional form. Here are the conjugations.

Haber – past subjunctive	Haber – conditional
yo hubiera	yo habría
tú hubieras	tú habrías
él, ella, lo, la hubiera	él, ella, lo, la habría
nos hubiéramos	nos habríamos
vos hubiérais	vos habríais
ellos hubieran	ellos habrían

The structure runs:
Si + hubiera + participle + habría + participle
More examples:
'Si hubiéramos cambiado de colegio habríamos hecho francés' – tf we had changed school, we would have taken French.
'Si hubieras hablado con él lo habrías entendido' – if you had spoken to him, you would have understood.

If statement alternatives

There are some alternative structures for if statements in second and third conditional. These are as follows.

Second Conditional
De + infinitive + conditional

For example:

'De saber la repuesta te la daría' – if I knew the answer, I would tell you.

'De estar de vacaciones, iría a la playa' – if I were on holiday, I would go to the beach.

Third Conditional
De + infinitive haber + participial + habria + participle

'De haber comprado un piso antes, habría pagada más – if I had bought a flat before, I would have paid more.

Another Third Conditional
Si + llegar (in present) + a + infinitive + habria + participle

'Si llego a estudiar para el examen habría aprobado' – if I had studied for the exam, I would have passed.

20. Making suppositions

A supposition is when a person takes in the facts at hand and makes an educated guess at what is probably real. For example, you see someone wearing a police uniform and driving a police car and you think 'she must be a police woman.'

The 'must' here is not for obligation (I must finish my homework) but rather for a supposition. In Spanish this type of sentence is made with:

Deber + de + infinitive

Therefore the above sentence would be:

'Debe de ser policía' and in negative 'ella no debe de ser policía, la vi robando un banco' – she can't be a police woman, I saw her robbing a bank.

For more information take a look at the Modals chapter here.

Suppositions in past

So far so good, but when it comes to the past it gets a little more tricky. You basically have three options. The first is to drop the 'de' and translate directly from English with the structure:

Deber + haber + participle in affirmative

And

No deber + haber + participle in negative

For example:

'Deben haber tenido sed ayer' – they must have been thirsty yesterday.
'No deben haber tenido calor' – they couldn't have been warm.

The second is to make 'deber' past with the structure:

Deber in past + de + infinitive in affirmative

And

No deber in past + de + infinitive in negative.

For example:

'Debió de volver a casa tarde' – he must have come home late.
'Debí de olvidarme las llaves, no están en el bolso' – I must have forgotten my keys, they aren't in my bag.

The final way seems the most strange to English speakers, but it is the most used. This is simply to use the **conditional tense** to express a probability. For example:
'¿Dónde estaba papá en aquel momento? Estaría en la cocina' – where was father in that moment? He was probably in the kitchen (or literally 'he would be in the kitchen').
'¿Cuántos años tenía la abuela entonces? Tendría unos 70 años' – how old was the grandmother then? She must have been about 70.
'No irían a la fiesta porque no tenían dinero para el autobús' – they couldn't have gone to the festival because they didn't have money for the bus (or literally 'they wouldn't go to the festival because they didn't have money for the bus.')
'¿Cuánto gastó en el coche?' 'Gastaría mucho' – how much did he spend on that car? He must have spent a lot (or literally, 'he would spend a lot').
'Debían de ser las once cuando cenamos' – it must have been about eleven when we had dinner.

Note: The conditional can also be translated as 'I wonder' + past. For example:
'¿Cuánto costaría el vestido que compró María?' – I wonder how much the dress that Maria bought, cost?
'I wonder' + present is with future tense, as I will explain below.

Future for probability in present

In the same way, if you want to talk about probability in present you use the future tense. For example, if someone calls you on your landline and you don't pick up in time, someone may ask you:

'¿Quién ha llamado?' – who called?

And you might answer:

'Será María' – it was probably Maria (or literally 'it will be Maria.')

More examples:

'¿Dónde está Juan?' 'Juan estará comiendo palomitas en el cine' – Where is Juan? Juan will probably be eating popcorn at the cinema.

'¿Cuánto costará un viaje a Brasil? – I wonder how much a trip to Brazil costs.

'Costará un ojo de la cara' – it will probably cost an arm and a leg.

Suponerse – to suppose

'Suponerse' can be translated as 'to suppose' in English. It is used to make suppositions just like English.

Its structure for present suppositions runs:

'Se supone' + que + indicative

And past suppositions

'Se suponía' + que + imperfect

In this way, instead of saying, 'you were supposed to' or 'she is supposed to' in the passive voice, you actually say 'It supposes that' in present and 'it is supposed that' in past. For example:

'Se supone que la comida está buena aquí' – the food is supposed to be good here (or literally, it supposes that the food is good here').

'Se suponía que el entrevista era una oportunidad' – the interview was supposed to be an opportunity (or literally, 'it is supposed that the exam was an opportunity')

'Se suponía que iba a volver el martes' – I was supposed to come back on Tuesday (or literally, 'it was supposed that I was going to come back on Tuesday.')

> **[Spanish/English Difference] Suppose**
>
> 'Suponerse', it is not used for obligation in the same way as 'to suppose' is in English. In Spanish, obligation is expressed with 'tener' or 'debería.' For example:
>
> 'Tengo que visitar a mi abuela este fin de semana' – I am supposed to visit my grandmother this weekend.
>
> 'No debería salir entre semana' – I am not supposed to go out in the week.

21. Ser versus Estar

There are two 'to be' verbs in Spanish, one for permanent characteristics 'ser' and one for impermanent things like emotions and physical states 'estar.' Working out whether to use 'ser' or 'estar' is one of the biggest problems English speakers face when learning Spanish but there are rules to help you.

Ser
The verb table for ser is:

I am	soy
you are	eres
he is	es
he is	es
it is	es
we are	somos
you are (plural, informal)	sois
you are (plural, formal)	son
they are	son

We use ser when:

It is the identity of the person or thing: 'Soy Ricardo', 'es parquet.'

The profession of someone: 'Julia es médica,' 'Juan es peluquero' – Juan is a hairdresser. Note that when referring to professions there is no article (un or una).

To describe things which are not likely to change: Such as characteristics of appearance and personality. 'Madrid es grande', 'el cielo es azul', 'los coches son caros,' 'Juana es alta', 'mi tía es simpática'.

Relationships between people: 'Éste es mi marido', 'ellos son mis hermanos', 'Julia es mi jefa' – Julia is my boss.

Price: '¿Cuánto cuestan los zapatos?' 'Son 25 euros,'

Time: 'Es la una' – it's one o'clock, 'son las ocho y media' – it's eight thirty.

Dates: 'Hoy es el ocho de marzo' – today is the 8th of March, 'mañana es viernes' – tomorrow is Friday.

With passive voice. 'El edificio fue construido hace 12 años' – the building was built twelve years ago.

Estar

The table for estar is:

I am	estoy
you are	estás
he is	está
she is	está
it is	está
we are	estamos
you (informal, plural)	estáis
you (formal, plural)	están
they	están

We use estar for:

Temporary moods: 'Estoy aburrido' – I am bored, 'estamos emocionados por la fiesta' – we are excited about the party, 'está preocupado por las notas' – he is worried about his marks.

Temporary physical states: 'Ella está malita hoy' – she is sick today, 'estoy cansado' – I am tired, 'estás muy delgado ahora mismo,' – you're very slim at the moment.

A temporary situation with the preposition 'de': 'Sara es abogada pero ahora está de camarera' – Sara is a lawyer but right now she is a waitress.

Location: 'El supermercardo está al lado de correos' – the supermarket is next to the post office. 'Madrid está a 400 km de la costa' – Madrid is 400 km from the coast.

In continuous tenses with 'ando' and 'iendo' to form the gerund (gerundio): 'Estoy mirando el cuadro' – I am looking at the painting or 'están jugando juntos' – they are playing together.

Expressions with estar

Estar a + date: This is another way to express the date.

'Estamos a cinco de marzo' – It is the 5th of March.

'Estar a punto de' + infinitive and 'estar para' + infinitive: To express something is about to happen.

'Estoy a punto de llamarte' – I am just about to call you.

'Está para comer' – he is about to eat.

Estar por + noun: To express what you are in favour of.

'Estamos por la democracia' – we are for democracy.

More expressions

'Estar de acuerdo' – to agree with

'Estar de vacaciones' – to be on holiday

'Estar de vuelta' – to be back. 'Todos están de vuelta' – they are all back

---

Adjectives that change their meaning with ser and estar

There are many adjectives that change their meaning depending on whether you pair them with 'ser' or 'estar.' Ser adjectives refer to the permanent characteristic of the thing while estar the impermanent state. English often does the same thing by changing the end of the adjective to 'ing' or 'ed.' For example: 'The film is boring.' This is the permanent characteristic of the film. In Spanish this is 'la película es aburrida.'

'I am bored by this film.' This is your impermanent state about how you feel about the film. In Spanish this is 'estoy aburrido por la película.'

Note, however, that adjectives ending in 'ante' are also permanent such as: 'El libro es interesante' – the book is interesting and 'estoy interesado en el libro' – I am interested in the book.

Adjectives with Ser and Estar

Ser aburrido – to be boring	Estar aburrido – to be bored.
Ser cansado – to be tiring	Estar cansado – to be tired.
Ser listo/a – to be clever	Estar listo/a – to be ready.
Ser malo – to be bad	Estar malo/a – to be ill.
Ser rico – to be rich	Estar rico – to be tasty.
Ser bueno – to be good	Estar bueno – to be tasty.
Ser seguro – to be safe	Estar seguro – to be sure.
Ser viejo – to be old	Estar viejo – to look old.
Ser vivo – to be sharp	Estar vivo – to be alive.
Ser dispuesto – to be willing	Estar dispuesto – to be prepared.
Ser fresco – to be cheaky	Estar fresco – to be fresh.
Ser grave – to be serious	Estar grave – to be seriously ill.
Ser interestado – To be selfish	Estar interestado – to be interested.
Ser molesto – To be annoying	Estar molesto – to be annoyed.
Ser negro – To be black	Estar negro – to be furious.
Ser verde – to be green	Estar verde – to be inexperienced.
Ser maduro – To be mature	Estar maduro – to be ripe.
Ser despierto – to be alert	Estardespierto – to be awake.
Ser pesado – to be heavy	Estar pesado – to be annoying.
Ser despierto/a – to be bright	Estar despierto/a – to be awake.
Ser inquieto – to be very active	Estar inquieto – to be worried.
Ser alegre – to be a joyful person	Estar alegre – to be merry (drunk).
Ser bueno/a – to be a good person	Estar bueno/a – to be attractive.

Ser violenta – to be violent   Estar violenta – to be embaressed/embaressing.

> **Common mistakes with ser and estar**
> **Ser for quanity and first, second, third...**
> If you turn up at a restaurant as a party of four you say to the waiter or waitress 'somos cuatro' using 'ser' and not 'estar' even though you are not permanently with these people.
> Likewise, if you turn up at the Correos (post office) and you see a queue of people, you ask 'quién es la última persona en la cola?' – who is the last person in the queue?' even though being the last or first at something is an impermanent state.
>
> **Estar for location**
> Even if someone or something has resided a particular place for many years you still use 'estar' to refer their location. The reason is that where they are changes in relation to you. For example, if you were to ask someone from Girona, Spain to tell you where Barcelona is they would say 'está hacia el sur' (it's towards the south) which is true from their perspective. However, if you were to ask someone from Valencia the same question they would say 'está hacia el norte' (it's towards the north) which is true for them also.
>
> **Estar for the price of fruit and vegetables**
> Though 'ser' is generally used for price, 'estar' is used when buying fruit and vegetables. That is because the price of these items changes from day to day, and so you would say:
> '¿A cuánto están las naranjas hoy?' – how much are the oranges today?
>
> **When it isn't ser or estar at all but tener**
> Sometimes when you're stressing about whether you need 'ser' or 'estar' you'll find it's neither of them but rather the verb 'tener'. 'Tener' (to have) is used in

many cases in Spanish where we would use 'to be' in English. Here are some examples:

Age: Tengo 30 años – I am 30.

States of hot or cold: 'Ella tiene frio, mientras él tiene calor' – she is cold while he is hot.

Note: There is no other way to express whether a person is hot or cold.

With the weather it is 'hace frío' or 'hace calor' – literally 'it makes hot or cold.' While with something inanimate that changes temperature such as water you use 'estar.' For example, 'el agua está fría hoy,' – the water is cold today.

Hunger and thirst: 'Tengo hambre' – I am hungry (or literally, I have hunger), 'ella tiene sed' – she is thirsty (or literally she has thirst).

To be scared/frightened: 'Tengo miedo' – I am scared (or literally 'I have fear').

To be in a hurry: 'Tengo prisa' – I am in a hurry (or literally 'I have hurry').

To be to blame for something: 'Él tiene la culpa del robo' – he is to blame for the robbery (or literally he has blame for the robbery').

To be right: 'Tienes razón' – you are right (or literally, 'you have reason').

Ser and estar in preterite and imperfect

After a bit of practice you start to make the distinction between 'ser' and 'estar' naturally. However, a further difficulty presents itself when you want to talk about the past as each verb can be split into preterite or imperfect meaning you now have four options for 'was'. These being: 'estuvo', 'estaba', 'fue' and 'era' (as well as all the conjugations).

Understandably this can cause a great deal of confusion, so here are a set of guidelines to help you make the distinction.

First of all, if the verb is 'ser' or 'estar' in present than it is still that verb in past tense. This means that all you have to think about is whether the verb is preterite or imperfect.

Estuve versus Estaba

Time: The preterite refers to a particular time in past and so if your sentence contains a past time marker such as 'la semana pasada' or 'ayer', 'estar' becomes 'estuve.'

If the sentence does not contain a time marker then it is usually in imperfect. For example:

'¿Dónde estabas?' 'la semana pasada estuvimos de vacaciones.'

'Estaban muy descontentos con las notas' or 'estuvieron muy descontentos con las notas el año pasado.'

Location: The imperfect expresses something that was true and continues to be true and so with things with a permanent location such as buildings use 'estaba', but with imperminent locations 'estuvo'. For example:

'¿Dónde estaba el taller de coches?' 'Estaba en Calle Rodrigo, y mi coche estuvo allí la semana pasada' – where was the mechanic's? It was in Calle Rodrigo and my car was there last week.

The past continuous tense: The past continuous tends to use the imperfect to emphasise the ongoing action.

For example:

'Juan estaba cocinando en la cocina mientras los niños estaban jugando en la sala.'

Fue vs era

In many ways the distinction between 'fue' and 'era' is more defined.

A life long characteristic: If the sentence refers to a permanent characteristic in the past of something or somebody then it is 'era.' For example:

'Ella era francesa, y muy trabajadora, pero sus nietos eran perezosos' – she was French and very hard working but her grandchildren were lazy.

Professions: With professions you would also use 'era' unless that profession only lasted a short period of time before the person changed it, in which case you would use 'fue.'

Time: The time is also with 'era.' For example, '¿cuándo era que le llamé?' 'Eran las 15.30h' – when was it that I called him? It was at three thirty.

Dates: Dates and days of the week, however, are with 'fue.'

Periods of time: If you're talking about something that happened over a long period of time, which has finished and carries a time marker, you use 'fue.' However, if you talk about something that happened for a long period without a time marker you use 'era'. Equally if you want to talk about the duration of the time with the adverb 'entre' (between) it is also with 'era'. For example:

'Julia fue mi jefa en 2008' – Julia was my boss in 2008.

'Julia era mi jefa' – Julia used to be my boss.

'Julia era mi jefa *entre* 1998 y 2008' – Julia was my boss between 1998 and 2008.

Prices: Prices would be with 'era', if the object is still that price or 'fue' if it was bought a long time ago and therefore would not be that price any more.

For example:

'¿Cuánto costaba la chaqueta que compraste la semana pasada?' 'Era $50, más barata que mi otra chaqueta que fue más cara,' – how much was the jacket you bought last week? It was $50, cheaper than my other jacket, which was more expensive.'

Note: If the sentence contains the item then use the verb 'costar' to describe the price. In the above sentence '¿Cuánto era la chaqueta?' is not correct.

Adjectives to describe events: As the event is finished then you use 'fue' to describe how you felt about it.

For example:

'La fiesta fue muy divertida la semana pasada' – the party was very fun last week.

'La película fue malísima' – the film was terrible.

Adjectives to provide a backdrop of a story: If the adjective forms the backdrop of a story, use 'era.' This happens particularly in literature.

For example:

'Era un día bonito cuando María salió de la casa' – it was a beautiful day when Maria left the house.

'Era una época muy dura y habían muchos pobres' – it was a very hard time and there were many poor people.

22. All the forms of haber

Think of all the forms of 'there'; 'there was', 'there has been', 'there could be', 'there could have been' and so on, well the same is true for 'haber.' Here are the possible combinations. In most cases you add an 'n' to make the verb plural ('habrán, habían and so on).

Note: 'h' in Spanish is not pronounced and so the pronunciation of 'hay' is 'eye'.

'Hay un coche en la calle' – there is a car in the street.
'Había un coche en la calle' – there was a car in the street.
'Antes había un coche en la calle' – there used to be car in the street.
'Habrá un coche en la calle' – there will be a car in the street.
'Va a haber un coche en la calle' – there is going to be a car in the street.
'Habría un coche en la calle' – there would be a car in the street.
'Ha habido un coche en la calle' – there has been a car in the street.

More 'hay' variations

'Puede que haya un coche en la calle'
'Es posible que haya un coche en la calle
'Quizás haya un coche en la calle'
} There may be a car in the street.

'Puede que haya habido un coche en la calle'
'Es posible que haya habido un coche en la calle'
'Quizás haya habido un coche en la calle'
'Habría un coche en la calle '
} There may have been a car in the street.

'Debería haber un coche en la calle' – there should be a car in the street.
'Debería haber habido un coche en la calle' – there should have been a car in the street (but there wasn't).

'Debe de haber un coche en la calle' – there must be a car in the street (because there was one there last night).
'Debe haber un coche en la calle' – there must be a car in the street (because it is an obligation).
'Debe de haber habido un coche en la calle' – there must have been a car in the street (strong speculation).
'Podría haber un coche en la calle' – there could be a car in the street.
'Podría haber habido un coche en la calle' – there could have been a car in the street.

May, might, should and could + there in past

Puede que + haya + habido + participle – there may have been.
'Puede que haya habido un premio' – there may have been a prize.
Podría + haber + habido – there could have been.
'Podría haber habido un acciente' – there could have been an accident.
Debería + haber + habido – there should have been.
'Debería haber habido una barrera' – there should have been a barrier.

23. The passive and its alternatives

There are two types of sentences in language; active and passive. For example:

Active	Passive
I ate the apple	The apple was eaten
They will finish the house	The house will be finished soon

In Spanish the passive is constructed with the structure:

Noun + ser + participle

If you want to add the person or thing doing the action (this is called the agent) add **'por' + name**.

The above sentences would be: 'la manzaña fue comido, por mí' and 'la casa será terminado pronto.'

Seems fairly easy right? Well don't get carried away because while we love this construction in English, it is rarely used in Spanish.

When to use object + ser + participle

This construction seems to be most used for important things that were created in the past and still exist today, particularly in the realm of art, literature, music, architecture or the founding of companies.

For example:

'Don Quijote fue escrito por Cervantes' – Don Quixote was written by Cervantes.

'Guernica fue pintado por Picasso' – Gernica was painted by Picasso.

'La empresa fue fundada en 1927' – The company was founded in 1927.

Estar and passive

'Estar' can be used for permanent states such as emotions. If you're speaking about more than one person or thing put the participle into plural. For example:

'Estaban emocionados por el viaje' – they were excited because of the trip.
'Las paredes fueron pintadas ayer' – the walls were painted yesterday.

Alternatives to the passive
Changing it back to active
Spanish is a very direct language and to speak well you really have to think like a native. The next time you have the urge to say 'the car was cleaned by my husband' or 'the report was finished yesterday'; reorder your sentence to make it active. The above sentence would therefore be changed to:
'Mi marido limpó el coche ayer' – my husband cleaned the car yesterday.
'Acabé el informe ayer' – I finished the report yesterday.

Changing the verb to reflexive
Changing the verb to reflexive makes a general 'you' or 'one,' for example:
'Se pueden pagar los impuestos ahora o la semana que viene' – you (one) can pay your (one's) taxes now or at the end of the week.
It also, however, makes a sentence passive. This is a strange idea at first but once you're used to it comes in very handy. These type of sentences in English would be constructed with either 'to be' verb + participle or 'to get' + participle. For example:
'El negocio se vendió hace tres años' – the business was sold three years ago (or literally 'the business sold itself three years ago).
'Las tiendas se abren a las 9.00h y se cierran a las 20.00h' – the shops are open at 9 o'clock in the morning and they are closed at 8 o'clock at night.
'Mi bolso se ha roto' – my handbag has got broken.
'No se enviará la carta' – the letter won't be sent.
'¿Dónde se encontró el cadáver?' – where was the body found?
'Se está construyendo una finca enorme en mi calle' – an enormous house is being built in my street.

When the passive refers to people

You cannot use the verb in reflexive in this way when the passive refers to people.

For example:

'El soldado se mató en la guerra' – instead of saying the soldier was killed in the war, you're saying he killed himself.

To avoid this problem put the appropriate indirect object pronoun between the 'se' and verb.

If the sentence includes a name (or word pertaing to a name 'soldado' 'rey', 'adolescente') then put 'a' in front of it. For example:

'Al soldado se le mató en la guerra' – the soldier was/got killed in the war.

'A Sofía se le promovió por la calidad de su trabajo' – Sofia got promoted because of the quality of her work. More examples:

'Se me dará una subida de sueldo en la primavera' – I will be given a pay rise in the spring.

'Se nos ha dicho que no habrá una huelga' – we have been told that there won't be a strike.

<u>Note:</u> The verb remains in singular even if the subject is plural.

'A Javier y Pilar se les arrestó en la calle' – Javier and Pilar were arrested in the street.

However, 'se' when referring to people can sound rather old-fashioned nowadays and it is more common to use an active sentence such as:

'Me regalaron un poni' – they gave me a pony.

'A Vincente le dijeron las notas' – they told Vicente about the marks.

24. Become and other verbs that express change

There are six verbs that express change in Spanish. These are: 'ponerse', 'hacerse', 'volverse', 'quedarse', 'llegar a ser' and 'convertirse' with each having their own slightly different meaning. This may seem excessive but what people tend to forget is English speakers also use a variety of verbs to express change. We have 'become', 'to get,' 'to go', 'to make', 'to turn' and 'to turn into.' Let's look at each one in more detail.

Ponerse
This means a sudden involuntary change in someone's mood, appearance or state of health. The change is temporary. Its closest relation in English is 'to get.' For example:
'Me pongo gordo cuando como chocolate y luego tengo que ponerme en forma' – I get fat when I eat chocolate and then I have to get fit.
'Ponerse' is also used when someone or something changes colour suddenly. In this way it would mean 'to turn.' For example:
'Cruzamos la calle cuando los semaforos se ponen en rojo' – we cross the street when the traffic lights turn red.
'Me pongo verde cuando vuelo en avión' – I turn green (sick) when I fly in a plane.'
Common adjectives used with ponerse: gordo/a, guapo/a (beautiful, when I make myself up) rojo/a, nervioso/a , enfermo/a (sick), furioso/a (furious), bien (better, after sickness), en forma (to get fit),triste (sad), contento/a (happy).

Ponerle
'Poner' can also mean 'to make' as in 'the film makes me sad'. In Spanish this is not the reflexive 'poner' but rather **indirect object + poner in third person.** For example:

'Los políticos le ponen furioso' – politicians make him furious.

'Me pone triste la película' – the film makes me sad.

Equally you could say 'he gets furious at the politicians' or 'I get sad at the film' which would be reflexive: 'Se pone furiouso con los políticos' or 'me pongo triste con la película.' More examples

'Mi familia me pone contento' – My family makes me happy.

'Poner las cosas difíciles a alguien – To make things difficult for someone.

Hacerse

Hacerse is used when there is a gradual change due to an effort. The change is normally permanent. It is most commonly used to express professions or beliefs. Its closest relation is in English is 'to become.' For example:

'Se ha hecho abodago' – he has become a lawyer (or literally 'he has made himself a lawyer').

'Se hizo rica' – she became rich (after many years of hard work).

It is also used with adjectives such as grande, mayor (old), alto/a (tall) to express a change in size, age or speed which is permanent. Its closest equivalent here is 'to get.' For example:

'Nos estamos haciendo mayores' – we are getting older.

'El internet en mi barrio se ha hecho más rapido' – The Internet in my neighbourhood is getting faster.

'Se hace alto tu hijo' – your son is getting tall.

Common adjecives used with hacerse: all professions, nationalities (if the person has changed it) belief systems such as liberal, ateo (atheist), rico, fuerte, gordo/a (to become fat over a long period of time), mayor, fuerte, debil, el dia (as in 'to get light when the sun comes up').

Volverse

'Volverse' indicates a fast, involuntary change that is often negative. The closest equivalent in English is 'to get.'For example:

'Se volvió loco cuando le despidieron' – he went crazy when they fired him.'
'Se ha vuelto tacaño' – he has become a stingy person.
If you suddenly get rich from the lottery you can also say 'se he vuelto rico por la lotería' – he got rich through the lottery.
Indirect object pronoun + volver in third person + loco also means to drive someone crazy.
'Los niños me vuelven loca hoy' – the kids are driving me crazy today.
Common adjectives used with volverse: insorportable (unbearable), antipático/a (unkind), 'loco/a' (crazy), 'rico/a' (rich, if it happened overnight) 'viral' (to go viral).

Quedarse

'Quedarse' expresses the loss of something or a change in physical appearance which is normally permanent and negative. For this reason it is often used for physical defects. Its closest equivalent in English is 'to go.' For example:
'Me padre se está quedando calvo' – my father is going bald.
'Preferiría quedarme sordo que ciego' – I would prefer to go deaf than blind.
'Me quedé en blanco cuando la maestra me hizo una pregunta' – I went blank when the teacher asked me a question.
Common adjectives used with quedarse: ciego/a (blind), sordo/a (deaf), cojo/a (lame), sin dinero (broke), en blanco (blank), calvo/a (bald), en la pobreza (thrown into poverty), embarazada (pregnant), viudo/a (widower, widow) and huérfano/a (orphan) sin palabras (to be left speechless) desesperante (desperate).

LLegar a ser

'Llegar a ser' ('arrive to be') means to become something over a period of time usually with effort. Its closest verb in English is 'to become.' For example:
'Llegó a ser periodista por estudiar por la noche en una academia' – he became a journalist by studying at night in an academy.

Convertirse en

'Convertirse en' means 'to turn into' in English, in other words to convert from one form to another. For example:

'La rana se convirtió en príncipe con un beso' –the frog turned into a prince with a kiss.

'La primavera se convierte en verano' – spring turns into summer.

It is also used for religious conversions with 'a' always going before the religion.

'Mi hermano se convirtió a protestante' – my brother became a protestant.

Other verbs to express change

Like English, Spanish has other verbs to express the start of something or provoking someone to do something.

Hacerle – to make someone do something

'Hacer' is used when the subject makes someone do something. For example:

'Me hace reír' – he makes me laugh.

'No me hagas trampas' – don't trick me.

'La película les hace llorar' – the film made them cry.

'Para hacerme sentir culpable' – to make me feel guilty.

'Hacer enfadar' – to make someone angry.

Echar – break into/ burst into

Echar means a sudden action which normally translates into 'to break' or 'to burst into' in English. Some examples include:

'Echar a llorar' – to burst into tears.

'Echar a correr' – to break into a run.

'Echar una bronca' – to suddenly tell someone off.

'Echar a reír' – to burst out laughing.

Ponerse – to start

Ponerse is another word for start. It is particularly used for machines. Examples include:

'Ponerse en marcha' – to start a machine.

'Me puse a limpiar la casa' – I started to clean the house.

'Me puse a reír' – I started to laugh.

'Ponerse a limpiar' – to start to clean.

'Ponerse a trabajar' – to get to work.

'Ponerse a llover' – to start to rain.

Cada vez más – increasingly

'Cada vez más' translates to 'increasingly' or 'getting' in English. For example:

'La vida es cada vez más cara' – life is getting more expensive.

'El dolor incrementa cada vez más' – the pain is getting worse.

When 'become' is within the verb

We have already learnt that 'to get + adjective' (as in 'to get sick') can be reasonably translated as 'ponerse'.

However, you cannot say 'ponerse enfadado' (angry) – you must instead say 'enfadarse' to anger oneself, using the reflexive form. For a list of verbs see The Reflexive chapter.

25. Whatever, no matter and ever

'Ever' words are everywhere in English. They exist in Spanish also, made with an interrogative adverb ('quién, cuándo, dónde and so on) and the verb in present subjunctive. For example:

'Llévales patatas fritas o lo que sea' – take the potato chips or whatever.
'Ven a la oficina cuándo quieras' – come to the office whenever you want.
'A donde vayamos siempre nos perdemos' – wherever we go, we always get lost
'Quien quiera la bolsa tiene que decírmelo ahora' – whoever wants the bag has to tell me now
'Llegaremos tarde con cualquier autobús que cojamos' – whichever bus we catch we will arrive late.
'¿Cómo quieres que cocine las verduras? 'Como quieras' – how do you want me to cook the vegetables? However you want.
Note: This is 'however' as in 'whatever way'. 'However' as in degree of something is 'por mucho' (see below).

Other forms of whenever
If you wish to say 'whenever' for repeated actions you use:
Siempre que + indicative
For example:
'Siempre que voy a Madrid me alojo en un hotel' – whenever I go to Madrid, I stay in a hotel.
'Siempre que envía un correo electrónico pone un emoticono' – whenever he sends an email he always puts an emoji.

Other forms of whatever
If you want to use 'whatever' to speak more generally then you use the structure:
Present subjunctive + lo que + present subjunctive

For example:

'Pase lo que pase la casa está pagada' - whatever happens the house is paid for.

'Diga lo que diga, no miento' – whatever they say I am not lying.

'Sea como sea no has terminado las obras aún – be that as it may you still haven't finished the roadworks.

However and no matter

However and no matter also express a degree of something. In Spanish this is:

Por mucho/a + verb in subjunctive or **por + adjective + verb**

For example:

'Por mucho frío que haga, voy a dar un paseo' – however cold it is I am going out for a walk

'Por mucho que te quejes vamos al teatro' – no matter much you complain we are going to the theatre.

'Por muy inteligentes que fueran, no mejoraron la economía' – however intelligent they were they didn't improve the economy.

'Por muy en forma que esté, no terminará el maratón' – however fit he is, he won't finish the marathon.

Whatsoever and at all

The closest equivalent to using 'whatsoever' and 'at all' to emphase a negative is 'en absoluto.'

For example:

'No me gusta correr en absoluto' – I don't like running whatsoever

'No come carne en absoluto' – she doesn't eat meat at all.

Not even and even

Not even

'Not even' as in 'not even my mother likes the cake,' is 'ni siquiera' or simply 'ni'. If you want to use 'not even' in its more emphatic form –such as, 'no one liked the party not even my brother,' put 'ni siquiera' at the end of the sentence. 'A nadie le gustó la fiesta, ni siquiera a mi hermano.'

However, if you want to use it in its lighter form you use 'ni' + verb. In English this is a auxiliary verb in negative + even. For example:

'Ni me invitaron a la boda' – They didn't even invite me to the wedding.

'No tenía ni un amigo en la universidad' – He didn't even have one friend at university.

'Preparamos la comida y ni nos llamaron para decir que llegarían tarde – We prepared the food and they didn't even call us to say they would arrive late.

Even

Positive 'even', on the other hand – such as 'today even I have money' is 'incluso'.

For example:

'Todo el mundo bailó, incluso mi abuela' – everyone danced, even my grandmother.

'Despedirán a todos los empleados, incluso al jefe' – they will fire all the workers, even the boss.

Expressions with 'ni'

'Ni' is also used in a couple of useful exclamations. Namely:

'¡Ni hablar!' – no way!

'¡Ni de broma!' – you're joking!

26. Reported speech

In both English and Spanish we use reported speech (also known as indirect speech) to recount what someone else says. For example:

One day our friend Maria says 'I **like** ice cream.' She is speaking directly to us and so it is therefore direct speech.

Later I recount what she said to my flatmate Andrew and say 'Maria said that she **liked** ice cream.' The mode of speech that I then use is indirect or reported speech.

In both languages there are tense changes when we recount what people say. Take the above example. When Maria speaks to me, she uses present tense. When I later recount the story to Andrew I use past tense.

This can be summed up in this table below. If you hear something in present tense you later recount it in imperfect tense. Equally, if you hear something in preterit tense you recount it in past perfect and so on.

Direct speech	Reported speech
Present or imperfect tense	Imperfect
Preterit or present perfect	Past perfect
Present continuous	Past continuous
Future or conditional	Conditional

Some examples:

Direct: Pablo: '¿Dónde están las llaves?'

Indirect: Pablo me preguntó dónde estaban las llaves. (Note there is no question or quote marks in reported speech).

Direct: Maria: Fuimos al supermercado y compramos cinco manzanas.

Indirect: Maria me dijo que había ido al supermercado y compraron cinco manzanas.

Direct: Pablo: Llamaré a Maria y pediré que venga con nosotros.'

Indirect: Pablo me contó que llamaría a Maria y le pediría que viniera con nosotros.

Other changes

Just as in English pronouns to change also.

Este, esta, esto (this) changes to ese, esa, eso, aquello, aquella, aquel (that).

Common reported speech verbs

Declarar – to declare.

Decir – to say.

Explicar – to explain.

Preguntar – to ask.

27. Adverbs

Still, already, yet, anymore

'Already','yet' and 'still' and 'anymore' are adverbs added to sentences to express if something has happened, hasn't happened (but will), continues to happen or used to happen but doesn't any longer.

In Spanish all these concepts are expressed with the two adverbs 'ya' and 'todavía,' depending on their placement in the sentence.

Already

In Spanish 'already' is expressed by 'ya', which you place either at the beginning of a sentence or at the end. Like English, it is most commonly used in the present perfect tense, but not exclusively so. For example:

'Ya han comido' – they have already eaten.

'Él ya ha visto la película' – he has already seen the film.

'Ya fue al partido' – he already went to the match.

'Ya sé la repuesta ' – I already know the answer.

Yet

'Yet' in English forms the negative and question. In Spanish this is 'ya' for the question and 'todavía' for the negative. 'Ya' usually goes after the verb and 'todavía'at the end of the sentence. Again, like English, it is most commonly used in present perfect.

For example:

'¿Has acabado ya los deberes?' – have you finished your homework yet?

'¿Ella ha encontrado ya las llaves?' – has she found her keys yet?

'No, ella no ha encontrado las llaves todavía' – no, she hasn't found her keys yet.

'No, no le he llamado todavía' – I haven't called him yet.

Still

'Still' means continuation. In Spanish this is expressed with either 'todavía', 'aún', or the verb 'seguir'. 'Seguir' is an irregular verb and follows the same pattern as 'pedir'. Like English, the Spanish 'still' is often used in either the present simple or continuous tense. It is placed either at the beginning or the end of sentences. For example:

'Estoy trabajando todavía' – I am still working.

'Ella vive aún en Barcelona' – She still lives in Barcelona.

'Él todavía está conduciendo' – He is still driving.

'Sigo estudiando español' – I am still studing Spanish.

Note that 'seguir' is followed by the verb in gerund without estar. For more on 'seguir' go to The Continuous chapter.

Anymore

'Anymore' means that something used to happen but doesn't now. In Spanish this is 'ya no' which is placed at the beginning of the sentence. For example:

'Ya no juegoal fútbol' – I don't play football anymore.

'Ella ya no fuma' – she doesn't smoke anymore.

'Ya no me hablas' – you don't speak to me anymore.

Just

'Just' has many meanings in English, but it is most commonly used to express something that happened in the recent past. In Spanish this is **acabar de + infinitive**. You conjugate acabar depending on whether it is for 'yo', 'tú,' él', 'ella' and so on but it is always in present tense. For example:

'Yo acabo de terminar el proyecto' – I just finished the project.

'Nosotros acabamos de comer' – we have just eaten.

'Ella acaba de encontrar trabajo' – she has just found work.

'Él acaba de dejar de fumar' – he has just given up smoking.

General Adverbs

Adverbs express how something happens. In English adverbs often end with 'ily' or 'ly,' such as 'she drives carefully' or 'he cooks wonderfully.' In Spanish adverbs often end with 'mente,' for example.

'Él habla italiano perfectamente' – he speaks Italian perfectly.

'Ella lee lentamente' – she reads slowly.

To do this you take the adjective, for example 'rápido,' and turn it into its feminine form ('ráida'), and then add 'mente' to make 'rápidamente'.

Note though you can't add 'mente' to all adjectives. A good rule of thumb is that if you can't add 'ly' to an adjective in English then you can't add 'mente' in Spanish. For example, you can say neither 'fatly' nor 'gordamente.'

When you have two adverbs

For two adverbs put the first into a feminine adjective and the second an adverb with 'mente.' For example:

'Ella habla suave y cuidadosamente' – she speaks softly and carefully.

'Él baila lenta y precisamente' – he dances slowly and precisely.

When you don't use mente

An alternative to 'mente' is **con** or **sin + adjective**. For example:

'Ellos patinan con cuidado' – they skate carefully (or literally 'they skate with carefulness').

'Trabajas sin prisa' – you work slowly (or without haste).

This is a very popular way to speak and is more common then then 'mente' form.

More examples:

'Ella juega con felicidad' – she plays happily/ she plays with happiness.

'Nosotros hablamos con cortesía' – we speak politely/ we speak with politeness.

'Cruza la calle sin cuidado' – she crosses the road without care.

'Quiero hablar contigo en serio' – I want to speak with you seriously

Adjectives that are also used as adverbs

Adjectives can also be use as adverbs in some cases in the masculine form. These include 'alto' ('high' or 'loud'), 'bajo' ('low' or 'softly'), 'fuerte' ('strongly' or 'hard'), 'claro' ('clearly') and 'rápido' ('fast').

Others are used in limited contexts – such as, 'jugar limpio' (to play fair/fairly),'ir derecho' (to go directly), 'respirar hondo' (to breathe deeply),'pensar distinto' (to think differently), 'costar barato o caro' (to cost a little or a lot).

Irregular adverbs

Like English there are also irregulars. These are:

Mal – badly: 'Ellos nadan mal' – They swim badly.

Bien – well: 'Ella habla bien inglés' – She speaks English well.

28. Some, any and nothing

Some and any in Spanish is 'algunos/as' or 'unos/unas' while nothing for this language function is 'ninguno/a'. It may be tempting to use these in exactly the same way as English but unfortunately in most cases they don't co-relate. Take a look below at the differences.

> **[Spanish/ English difference] Some and any for plurals**
> As an English speaker it is tempting to put the equivalent of 'some' or 'any' before plural nouns to express quantity but Spanish doesn't work that way. To understand this properly first we need to look at how we use 'some' and 'any' in English.
>
> **Plurals**
> For plurals in English we put a 'some' or 'any' before the noun depending on whether it is affirmative, negative or a question. For example:
> 'Do you have any socks?' and 'yes I have some socks.'
> In Spanish, however, you would only use unos, unas, algunos, algunas if the quantity of the thing you were referring to were important, maybe because you were surprised to see that quantity or maybe because you expected more. Otherwise you omit them entirely. You can imagine this as figuratively putting 'some' and 'any' in *italics*. For example:
> '¿Hay vasos en la mesa?' – are there any glasses on the table? 'Sí, hay vasos en la mesa' – yes there are some.
> 'No, no hay vasos en la mesa' – no there aren't any.
> In this whole conversation the speakers did not care how many glasses there were on the table they just wanted to communicate yes or no.
> Now imagine that the speakers are preparing for an important dinner party and they are running late. Suddenly the quantity of glasses becomes important. Now the conversation would run:

'¿Hay vasos en la mesa?' – are there *any* glasses on the table?

'Sí, hay algunos en la mesa' – yes there are *some* (as in 'would you like me to lay more?')

[Spanish/ English difference II] Some and any with uncountable nouns

In English we place 'some' and 'any' before uncountable nouns. An uncountable noun is something that can't be counted or made plural such as air, water, traffic, snow and so on. (For more about countable and uncountable nouns see the How much, how many chapter.)

Spanish, however, does not allow 'some' and 'any' before uncountable nouns. For example,

'Hay unos aire en el globo' (there is some air in the ballon) is completely wrong. The correct version is 'hay aire en el globo,' omitting the article entirely.

More examples

'Tengo agua en el bolso, ¿quieres?' and 'No, ¿pero tienes fruta?'

'¿Hay pan hoy?' – is there any bread today?

Alguno

There is the singular pronoun 'alguno.' Not to be confused with 'algún', 'algunos', 'algunas,' it means 'one' rather than 'some.'

For example:

'¿Hay alguno de tus amigos que sepa como llegar a la estación?' – is there one of your friends who knows how to get to the station?

'¿Hay algún niño que pueda contester esta pregunta?' – is there one child who can answer this question?

Singular nouns

Singular nouns are treated in much the same way as they are in English, placing an 'un' or 'una' before the noun whether it is an affirmative, negative or question.

For example:

'Hay un gato en la cama pero no hay un perro' – there is a cat on the bed but there isn't a dog.

Negatives

For a plural negative (when the quantity is important) you use 'ninguno' and 'ninguna' depending on the gender of the noun. So the case of the dinner party; if there were no glasses you would say:

'No, no hay ninguno' – no there aren't *any* (as in 'what a disaster! I'll get some from the cupboard').

Note: Use of ningunos and ningunas is also possible for plural nouns but it is not common.

Finally, this can be summed up in the following table:

	Affirmative	Negative	Question
A/an	un/una	un/una	un/una
Some/any (plural, if quantity matters)	algunos/unos/as	ninguno/a	algunos/unos/as
Some/any (uncountable)	n/a	n/a	n/a

Expressing quantities: Nada, ninguno, nadie y nada

'Nada' means 'nothing' and 'anything' in negative sentences. For example:

'Ellos no saben nada' – they don't know anything.

'No hay nada que puedas hacer' – there is nothing that you can do or there isn't anything that you can do.

It is also used in the phrase 'de nada,' meaning 'you're welcome,' and 'no pasa nada,' meaning 'don't worry about it.'

Ninguno, ninguna, ningún

'Ningún', 'ninguno' and 'ninguna' means 'none', 'not any' or 'no.' 'Ninguno' and 'ninguna' are pronouns for masculine and feminine nouns respectively while 'ningún' is an adjective that is placed before singular masculine nouns.

For example:

'No hay ninguno' – there aren't any.

'No tiene ninguna' – he doesn't have any/ he has none.

'Ningún niño sabe la repuesta' – none of the children know the answer.

'Ningún coche es azul' – none of the cars are blue.

'No quiero ningún problema en la reunión' – I don't want any problem in the meeting.

'Ellos no poseen ningún libro' – they don't own any books.

'En ningún momento dijo nada' – at no moment did he say anything.

Ninguno, ninguna – Neither and either

'Ninguno/a' also means a choice of a few people or things in negative. In English this would be expressed with 'either' or 'neither' – however, while 'either' and 'neither' mean only a choice of two, 'ninguno/ a' can mean more by adding 'de los tres', 'de los cuantro' or 'de las cinco' and so on. For example:

'Ninguno de los dos ha recibido el paquete' – neither of them has received the package.

'Ninguna de las tres chicas sabe cantar' – neither of the three girls knows how to dance.

'Ella no quiso ninguna de los galletas' – she didn't want either of the biscuits.

'A nosotros no nos gusta ninguna de las películas' – we don't like any (or either, if it's between a choice of two) of the films.

Note that after ninguno/a, the verb remains in third person singular, even if you're speaking about many people or things. This is the same in English for example, 'neither of them wears a tie' which would be 'ninguno de los dos lleva una corbata.'

And finally

Ningunos and ningunas are possible as pronouns for plural nouns but they are hardly used in Spanish as 'ninguno/a' can be used instead.

Nadie – no one and not anyone

Nadie means 'no one', 'nobody' and 'anyone' and 'anybody.' Just like English, the following verb is in singular, third person. For example:
'Nadie sabe cocinar en esta casa' – no one knows how to cook in this house.
'No hablé con nadie en la fiesta' – I didn't speak to anybody at the party.
'Nadie está comprando huevos hoy' – no one is buying eggs today.
'No hay nadie que pueda reparar este coche' – there isn't anyone who can repair this car.

Spanish quanities can be summed up in this table:

	Singular masculine	Singular femenine	Plural
some	alguno/algún	alguna	algunos/as
a/an	uno/ un	una	unos/unas (some)
none/not any/no	ninguno/ningún	ninguna	ningunos/ningunas
neither/either (can refer to more than two)	ninguno	ninguna	-
nothing	Nada	nada	nada

For some clarification on the 'none', 'not any', 'neither', 'either' question, take a look at these translations.

'Ninguno de los dos ha hecho los deberes' – neither of them have done their homework.

'A ninguno de la clase le gusta las matemáticas' – none of the class likes maths.

'No quiero ninguna de las dos bebidas' – I don't want either of the drinks.

'No ha terminado ninguna de las tareas' – she hasn't finished any of the tasks.

Tampoco

To agree in the negative with someone you use the word 'tampoco' usually at the beginning of the sentence. This is 'neither' or 'either' in English. For example:

'A mí tampoco me gusta peliculas de miedo' – I don't like horror movies either.

'Él tampoco ha aprobado el examen' – He hasn't passed his exam either.

Note: in Spanish you don't put 'no' before the verb as 'tampoco' makes the sentence negative.

29. How much, how many and other quantities

Cuántos y cuánto – how many and how much

How many

'How many' is for things that you can count – for example, 'how many tomatoes are in the fridge?' or 'how many siblings does she have?

In Spanish this is 'cuántos' for masculine nouns and 'cuántas' for feminine. For example:

'¿Cuántos coches tiene tu hermana?' – how many cars does your sister have?
'¿Cuántas sillas hay en el comedor?' – how many chairs are there in the dining-room?

How much

'How much' is for things that are uncountable, such as 'money', 'air', 'water', 'chocolate' and so on. In Spanish this is 'cuánto' or 'cuánta' depending on whether the noun is masculine or feminine. For example:

'¿Cuánto dinero cuesta?' – how much money does it cost?
'¿Cuánta agua bebes cada día?' – how much water do you drink each day?

When a noun is countable and when it isn't

Generally speaking, Spanish and English are the same when judging whether something is countable or not.

Liquid is uncountable in both languages unless it is in a container such as 'a cup of coffee.' In addition, so is 'fruta', 'carne' ('meat') arroz ('rice') and 'pan'. 'Verduras' ('vegetables') is countable in both languages.

[Spanish/English Difference] Countable and uncountable nouns

There are, however, some notable differences where a noun is countable in Spanish where it would be uncountable in English and vice versa:

Uncountable nouns cuánto, cuánta	Countable nouns cuántos, cuántas
La gente – the people La ropa – the clothes	Los deberes – homework los muebles – the furniture Los datos – the data Los consejos – the advice Las noticias – the news Todos/todas – everybody Las tostadas – the toast

Note: It is 'La gente es rica' – the people is rich not, 'la gente son ricos' – the people are rich. This is a very common mistake.

When a noun can be both countable and uncountable

There are many nouns that can be either countable or uncountable depending on the context. For example, 'how much chocolate do you eat?' (referring to the general concept of chocolate) and 'How many chocolates do you eat' (referring to a collection of chocolates in a box).

This is exactly the same in Spanish. You can say '¿cuánto café bebe?' – how much coffee does he (generally) drink?' and '¿cuántos cafés bebe?' – how many coffees does he drink? (say, in a day).

Other nouns where this applies include 'cerveza/cervezas' ('beer', 'beers'), 'ejercicio/ejercicios' ('exercise', 'exercises'), 'azúcar'/'azúcares' ('sugar', 'sugars') and so on. You get the picture.

How to answer adverbs of quantity: 'mucho', 'muchos', 'poco' and 'pocos'

Now we've talked about the question, let's go onto answer.

Just as in English, your answer will use a countable or uncountable adverb depending on whether it was a 'cuánto/a' or 'cuántos' question. In Spanish it's exactly the same.

| Cuánto/a | Cuántos/as |
| (Uncountable adverbs) | (Countable adverbs) |

↑ Mucho/a - A lot	↑ Muchos/as – A lot
Bastante – Quite a lot	Bastante – Quite a lot
↓ Un poco/a – A little	↓ Unos pocos/as – A few

For example:

'¿Cuánta fruta comes?', 'Como mucha fruta' – how much fruit do you eat? I eat a lot of fruit.

'¿Cuántos cafés bebes durante el día?', 'Bebo pocos cafés durante el día' – how many coffees do you drink a day? I drink a few coffees a day.'

Note that 'mucho' and 'muchos', 'poco' and 'pocos' are masculine and change gender ('muchas', 'pocas' etc.) depending on the gender of the noun.

More examples

'Ella hace bastante ejercicio a la semana' – she does quite a lot of exercise a week.

'Le pagan bastante' – they pay him quite a lot.

'Después de un poco vino estamos borrachos' – after a little wine we are drunk.

'Tengo unas pocas monedas en el bolsillo mientras que él tiene muchas' – I have a few coins in my pocket while he has many (lots).'

Todo/a and todos/as – All, everything and everybody

'Todo/a' means 'everything' or 'all' for uncountable nouns while 'todos/as' means the same for countable ones. They change ending depending on the gender of the noun. When speaking about routine Spanish speakers use 'todos' to mean 'every.' For example:

'Todas mis amigas saben tocar instrumentos' – all my friends know how to play instruments.
'Todo es un desastre' – everything is a mess.
'Todos los domingos como con mi familia' – every Sunday I eat with my family.
'Él cuida a todos los niños' – he takes care of all of the children.

Other uses of todos

'Todos' also means everybody. But be careful, while 'everybody' is singular in English ('everybody is watching the football match') in Spanish it is plural ('todos están viendo el partido de fútbol'). This is the exact opposite of 'la gente' (the people) which is singular in Spanish and plural in English. 'La gente está hablando' – 'The people are talking.'

Todo el mundo

'Todo el mundo,' which literally means 'all the world,' is the other way to say 'everybody' and is singular. For example:
'A todo el mundo le gusta la libertad' – everybody likes freedom.
'Todo el mundo conoce por lo menos una buena persona' – everybody knows at least one good person.

Otro/a y otros/as – another and others

'Another' and 'other' are both 'otro' in Spanish. If you say 'un otro café por favor' you are literally saying 'an another coffee please' – this is a very common mistake. Likewise 'otros' is used for plural which would be 'others' in English. They change ending depending on the gender of the noun. For example:

'Quiero otro libro' – I want another book.

'Tengo una carta aquí, ¿dónde está la otra?' – I have one letter here, where is the other (one)?

'Tenemos botas negras a la venta pero hay otras si quieres probarlas' – we have black boots on sale but there are others if you want to try them.

'Hay otros problemas en el mundo aparte de tu coche' – there are other problems in the world apart from your car.

Negative lists with 'ni'

If you have a list of things you don't want or like then you use 'ni.' For example:

'Ella no quiere llevarse ni la camiseta gris ni la azul' – she doesn't want to wear either the grey t-shirt or the blue one.

'No beben ni cerveza ni vino, son casi abstemios– they don't drink either beer or wine they are practically teetotal.

30. Too, enough, so much, so many, so

Demasiado – Too, too much, too many

'Too' means more than is needed and in English it is 'too much', 'too many' and 'too' depending on whether it is paired with a countable or uncountable noun or an adjective. In Spanish it is a lot simpler; it is 'demasiado' in all of the above cases.

For example:

'Es demasiado tarde para hacer los deberes' – it is too late to do your homework.

'Hay demasiado tráfico esta mañana' – there is too much traffic this morning.

'Ella tiene demasiados problemas' – she has too many problems.

'Ellos están demasiado cansados para ir al cine' – they are too tired to go to the cinema.

Enough - Suficiente

'Enough' in Spanish is 'suficiente' when followed by a noun or 'suficientemente' when followed by an adjective. For example:

'Tengo suficiente dinero' – I have enough money.

'¿Tienes chocolate suficiente? – do you have enough chocolate?

'¿Está la comida lo suficientemente caliente?' – is the food hot enough?

'El coche no es lo suficientemente grande' – the car isn't big enough.

'Bastante,' also means 'enough' in affirmative (it is not normally used in the negative or in questions). For example:

'Tengo bastante gasolina' – I have enough petrol (or gas)/ I have quite a lot of petrol.

'El ordanador va bastante rápido' – the computer is fast enough/ the computer is quite fast.

'Tiene bastante agua' – she has enough water/ she has quite a lot of water.

However, be careful here as 'bastante' can also mean 'plenty,'so can seem boastful.

'Tengo bastante dinero' means 'I have plenty of money' and to a lesser extent 'I have enough money.'

If you want to say 'I have enough money and no more than that, 'it would be 'Tengo suficiente dinero.'

So much, so many

'So much' (used for uncountable nouns) is 'tanto' or 'tanta' while 'so many' (used for countables is) 'tantos' or 'tantas'. For example:

'Ellos comen tanta carne y tantas tortillas' – they eat so much meat and so many tortillas.

The negative is made with 'no' and the comparative with 'como.' For example:

'No hay tanto tráfico como ayer' – there isn't as much traffic as yesterday.

'No tiene tantos amigas en este colegio como en el último' – she doesn't have as many friends in this school as she did in the last one.

So and such

So

'So' is 'tan' or 'tanto' in Spanish and goes before an adjective. For example:

'Hace tanto calor hoy que estoy sudando' – it is so hot today, I am sweating.

It is also used to make comparisons. This would be with 'as' in English.

'No es tan listo como su primo' – he isn't as clever as his cousin.

'España no es tan rica como Estados Unidos' – Spain isn't as rich as the USA.

Such

Broadly speaking 'such' translates to 'semejante' in Spanish with the structure **verb + semejante + noun.** For example:

'Tiene semejante caradura al pedirme este favor' – she has such a nerve to ask me this favour.

'Jamás diría semejante tontería' – I would never say such a stupid thing.

Poco/pocos – not much/not many

'Poco/a' means 'not much' or 'not very', while 'pocos/as' means 'not many'. This can be confusing because 'un poco' means 'a little' or 'quite' meaning that if you add an 'un' you're saying the exact opposite.

Take a look at these examples:

'He estudiado poco' – I haven't studied much (and I should study more).

'He estudiado un poco' – I have studied a little (I feel prepared).

'Mi amigo es poco inteligente' – my friend isn't very intelligent.

'Mi amigo es un poco inteligente' – my friend is a quite intelligent.

'Hay poco gente que venga a la fiesta' – not many people are coming to the party.

'Hay pocos lugares donde podamos ir sin coche' – there are not many places where you can go without a car.

31. Prepositions

There are not as many prepositions in Spanish as there are in English, and if you can learn which go with certain verbs then you are well on your way to mastering the language. First let's look at a common cause of confusion among English speakers: para vs por.

Para vs por

'Para' and 'por' both mean 'for' in English but there are some important distinctions between the two.

Para

Think of 'para' like an arrow going towards a destination. In this way it can mean either 'to' or 'for' in English. For example, you buy a present but who is it for? (or 'going to'):

'El regalo es para John' – the present is for John.

You receive a new table cloth but where is it for? (or 'going to'):

'El mantel es para la cocina' – the table cloth is for the kitchen.

Uses of para:

A purpose: In English this would be with 'to' or 'in order to'. In Spanish it is **para + infinitive**.

'Compraré una aspiradora para limpiar la casa' – I will buy a vaccum cleaner to clean the house.

'¿Qué quieres para comer?' – what do you want to eat?

'Ella ahorra dinero para comprar un nuevo ordenador' – she saves money in order to buy a new computer.

The recipient of something:

'He comprado tres entradas de cine para nosotros' – I have bought three cinema tickets for us.

A final destination: If you want to speak about where you finally end up on your travels you could use para.

'Fuimos para Córdoba la semana pasada' – we went to Córdoba las week.
'Salimos para el colegio a las ocho y media' – we leave for school at eight thirty.
Deadline: It is used to express a final time limit or deadline in the future.
'Tengo que terminar el informe para el viernes' – I have to finish the report for (or before) Friday.
Standard: If something is different from the standard you use 'para' to make the comparison.
'Para ser un libro del colegio es muy corto' – for a school book it's very short.
'Las habilidades la lectura de su hija son muy avanzadas para su edad' – your daughter's reading skills are very advanced for her age.
Opinion: 'Para' is also translated as 'in my opinion.'
'Para mí el trimestre es demasiado largo' – in my opinion the school term is too long.
'Para ellos el fútbol es aburrido' –in their opinion football is boring.
To express whether someone is in the mood for something:
'No estoy para bromas hoy' – I am not in the mood for jokes today.
'Está (de humor) para jugar hoy' – he is in the mood for playing today.
'No están (de humor) para discutir – they are not in the mood for arguing.
'Está para tenis hoy' – he is in the mood for tennis today.

Por

'Por' expresses many ideas, all of which are included below.

Uses of por:

For mañana ('morning'), tarde, día y noche: 'Por' is used to express what part of the day something happens. This would be 'in' or 'at' in English.
'Él trabaja por el día y estudia por la noche' – he works in the day and studies at night.
'Mañana por la mañana jugamos a tenis' – tomorrow morning we will play tennis.

To mean or 'at around about' when speaking about time:

'Te veo por las cinco' – I'll see you around 5.

'Llega por las seis' –he will arrive at about six.

The exchange of something: 'Por' also means an equal exchange or a substitute.

'Te doy una manzana por una pera' – I will give you an apple for (in exchange for) a pear.

'Han pagado 50 euros por la comida' – they have paid 50 euros for (in exchange for) the food.

'Hablo por mi jefe hoy' – I am speaking for my boss today (as a substitution).

Emotions: If you have an object for someone (such as a pencil) then you use para. If it is an emotion then it is with 'por.' This is also the case when saying thank you.

'Tengo mucho respeto por Maria' – I have a lot of respect for Maria.

'Gracias por venir a la fiesta' – Thanks for coming to the party.

Motivation: 'Por' is also actually short for 'porque' (because) and so expresses the motivation for doing something. In English this would be 'because of' or 'due to.' The structure is **por + infinitive**.

'Por aprender inglés ha conseguido el trabajo' – due to learning English, he got the job.

'Es más feliz por terminar los exámenes' – she is happier due to finishing her exams.

'Está deprimida por perder el perrito' – she is depressed because of losing her dog.

'Pablo tiene éxito por su personalidad' – Pablo is successful because of his personality.

Por for 'by'

'Por' means 'by' in the cases of 'by someone' or 'by phone'.

'Las Mellizas fue pintado por Velázquez' – Las Mellizas was painted by Velazquez.

'Oliver Twist fue escrito por Dickens – Oliver Twist was written by Dickens.

'Te lo enviaré por fax' – I will send it to you by fax.

Use of 'por' for electronics:

Por ordenador – by computer.

Por correo electrónico – by email.

Por correo – by mail.

Por fax – by fax.

Por teléfono – by telephone.

Por Internet – on the internet.

NOTE: With Internet it is not precided by the indefinite article ('the') and it is always with 'por', for example:

'Buscaba anoche por Internet' – I was searching on the Internet last night.

Por sayings

There are many sayings with 'por'. Here are the most popular:

Por allí – around there.

Por aquí – around here.

Por ejemplo – for example.

Por eso – for that reason.

¡Por fin! – finally!

Por lo general – in general.

Por lo menos – at least.

Por primera vez – for the first time.

Por seperado – separately.

Por supuesto – of course.

Por todas partes – everywhere.

The personal a

In Spanish you always put an 'a' before a person if they are the receiver of the action (or the direct object) in a sentence. For example:

'Mi madre cuida a mi hijo entre semana' – my mother looks after my son in the week.

In this sentence there are two people, (mi madre y mi hijo). Mi madre is the provider of the action (and so therefore the subject) and mi hijo the receiver (and so therefore the object). Therefore the 'a' goes before 'hijo'. More examples:

'¿Has llamado a Maria?' – have you called Maria?

'Compraré a Paula un regalo para su cumpleaños' – I will buy Paula a present for her birthday.

Note: If the sentence was reordered to make the 'regalo' the direct object 'para' would go before the person.

'Compraré un regalo para Paula para su cumpleaños.'

The personal 'a' is also used for pets or domestic animals that hold an emotional significance. For example:

'Sofia toca a su gatito' – Sofia strokes her cat.

It is not used for objects or animals which are not emotionally significant. For example:

'Pedro pone las gallinas en el gallinero' – Pedro puts the hens in the hen house.

Once you get used to using the personal 'a' it actually makes things easier as when it comes to people you don't have to fret about which preposition to use with the verb.

Verbs that have a different preposition in Spanish than they do in English

You're a language genius so don't learn the prepositions for *every* verb, only learn the ones that use a different one in Spanish.

To arrive at – llegar a.
To be astonished by – asombrarse de.
To bump into something – tropezar con.
To depend on – depender de.
To be dressed in – vestirse de.
To care for – cuidar de.
To consist of – consistir en.
To crash into – chocar contra.
To be covered with – cubrir de.
To dream about – soñar con.
To fill with –Llenar de.
To get married to – casarse con.
To happen to someone/something – pasarle a alguien/algo.
To look like someone – parecerse a.
To relate to, to do with – relacionarse con.
To sound like – sonar como.
To smell like – oler a.
To be surprised at – sorprenderse de.
To taste like – saber a.
Take time to do something – tardar tiempo en.
To think about – pensar en.

Part II
How do you say?

This part of Spanish for Geniuses opens the door onto the way Spanish speakers really speak with phrases and tip bits to make thousands of conversations from chatting with friends, organising, negotiating, receiving a service or solving an emergency. You need it? You'll find it here.

A word on politeness

Learners should take note that there is a large difference between South America and Spain in what is an acceptable way to speak. In South America, if you don't know someone well (such as waiting staff) or or older people, you must use the 'usted' form of the verb. In Spain, however, it is perfectly normal to use tú for people you both know and don't know. 'Usted', however, is still normally used for the elderly.

32. Speaking about time

How long have you...?

Communicating how long something has been happening is most commonly done in present tense. As this is often hard for English speakers to remember, let's recap a moment.

The question 'how long have you bee doing something' comes in three forms.

¿Cuánto tiempo hace que + present...?

¿Desde cuándo' + present...? (literally since when)

¿Desde hace cuánto tiempo + present...?

For example:

'¿Cuánto tiempo hace que tienes esa camiseta?' – how long have you had that t-shirt for?

'¿Desde cuándo trabaja para la empresa tu hermano?' – how long/ since when has your brother worked for the company?

'¿Desde hace cuánto tiempo vives aquí? – how long have you been living here for?

Answering

Your answer to any of these questions would be with **present + desde hace + time**. 'Desde hace' means 'for'.

For example:

'Tengo esta camiseta desde hace mucho tiempo' – I have had this t-shirt for a long time.

Desde que

Desde que + past means 'since' if the action continues to the present.

For example:

'Desde que ganó el partido en diciembre el Real Madrid ha estado a la cabeza de la liga' – since that they won, Real Madrid have been at the head of the league.

How long have you been + gerund
In English we often put this question into continuous form to emphasise the action. For example, the question 'how long have you been working here?' has more life than the question 'how long have you worked here?'
Spanish does the same with the verb **llevar + present continuous**.
For example:
'Llevo esperando en la estación cuatro horas' – I have been waiting at the station for four hours.
'¿Cuánto tiempo llevas esperando aquí?' – How long have you been waiting here for?
'Llevamos viviendo aquí diez años' – We have been living here for ten years.

How long had you been?
'How long had you been…?' asks about something that started in the past, went on for a time and then ended in the past. In Spanish this is:
Cuánto tiempo hacía que + verb in imperfect
Or
Hacía cuánto tiempo que + verb in imperfect
For example:
'¿Cuánto tiempo hacía que trabajabas aquí antes de conocer a tu mujer?' – how long had you been working here before you met your wife?
The answer would also be in imperfect with the structure:
Hacía + expression of time + que + verb in imperfect
Or
Verb in imperfect + desde hacía + expression of time
For example:

'Hacía seis meses que trabajaba aquí antes de conocer a mi mujer' – I had been working here for six months before I met my wife.

'Había estado yendo a la clase de cerámica desde hacía dos meses antes de darme cuenta de que no me gustaba – I had been going to my pottery class for two months before I realised I didn't like it.

Speaking about a single event in the past

If you want to express a past event that took place at a specific time (ago) use the preterite tense with this structure:

Hace + expression of time + que + verb in preterite

For example:

'Hace cinco años que me rompí la pierna' – five years ago I broke my leg.

Past prepositions: Durante vs Por

'Durante' and 'por' both mean 'for' with time. When speaking about the past use 'durante' and when talking about the future use 'por'. For example:

'Fui al colegio durante quince años' – I went to school for fifteen years.

'Vamos de vacaciones por dos semanas' – we are going on holiday for two weeks.

However, after verbs such as vivir, estar, esperar the 'for' is omitted all together.

Tardarse – to take for time

For questions such as 'How long does it take you to get ready in the morning?' you use 'tardarse'. However, be careful, in Spanish it is not 'it takes me' but rather 'I take myself'. For example the sentence above would be:

'Me tardo dos horas en prepararme por las mañanas.'

'Se tardó tres horas en llegar a la ciudad' – it took him three hours to get to the city.

'Se han tardado mis padres cinco horas en preparar la comida así que comedlo todo por favor' – it has taken my parents five hours to prepare the meal so eat everything please.

Note: It is 'en' before the infinitive verb.

Questions and answers with tardarse

The question is **cuánto tiempo + tardar + en + infinitive.** If you wish to ask 'how much longer..? (as in 'how much longer before something happens?') it would be 'cuánto tiempo más' or 'cuánto falta.' For example:

'Cuánto falta hasta navidad?' – how much longer until Christmas?

For answers to 'tardar' questions use the adverb 'mucho.' Unlike English you don't have to combine this with the noun 'tiempo.' For example:

'Cuánto tiempo te tardas en va al colegio en pie? – how long does it take you to walk to school?

'No me tardo mucho. 10 minutos, nada mas pero me tardo mucho en ir al fútbol' – it doesn't take me long, 10 minutes only but it does take me a long time to go to football.

How to say the date

Los días de la semana – Days of Week

Dates of the week are expressed with 'el' + day and for multiple days 'los'. They are not capitalised.

La fecha – The date

Compared to English the date ('la fecha') is easy. Spanish dates use cardinal numbers (one, two, three and so on) and the months are masculine.

The date is therefore:

El + number + de + month

For example: 'Hoy es el dos de abril' – today is the 2nd of April.

Adding the year

This is where it gets complicated. Spanish years are expressed by thousands. For example, the year 1981 would be 'mil novecientos ochenta y uno'. '2010' would be 'dos mil diez'

Spanish/English difference: Dates

Unlike English there is no 'and' between the thousand and the decimal.

And so a complete date would be:

'Era el dieziocho de diciembre de dos mil cinco' – it was the 14th of december 2005.'

NOTE: The second 'de' comes before the year.

An easy way to say the year

Because saying the year is such a mouthful, Spanish speakers often only refer to it in its decade with the structure:

En + el + año + number

For example:

'Aprobé mi examen de conducir en el año noventa y nueve' – I passed my driver's test in '99.

'Se casaron en el año setenta y seís' – they got married in '76.

Date questions

This is **cuál + ser + la fecha**. For example:

'¿Cuál es la fecha de hoy?' – what is the date today? (Literally, which is the date today)

Or

'¿Cuál era la fecha de ayer?' –what was the date yesterday?

How to say the time...

The time in Spanish is expressed with 'la,' which refers to 'la hora' (the hour) and the verb 'ser.' When the hour is singular (for one o'clock) it is **es + la** and the rest of the time **son + las**. For example:

'Es la una' – it's one o'clock.

'Son las dos' –it's two o'clock.

Minutes are added with 'y'. This would be 'past' in English.

'Es la una y veinticinco' – it's twenty-five minutes past one.

'Son las seis y diez' –it's ten minutes past six.

Minutes can be taken away from the following hour using the word 'menos' ('less'). This would be 'to' in English.

'Es la una menos vente' –it's twenty to one.

'Son las cuatro menos cinco' –it's five minutes to four.

Half past and quarter past

'Es la una y media' –it's half past one.

'Son las tres y cuarto' – it's quarter past three.

'Son las cinco menos cuarto' –it's quarter to five.

Specific times

To say something occurs at a specific time, use the structure:

A + la(s) + time

'El colegio empieza a las nueve' –school begins at nine o'clock.

'El restaurante abre a las once y media' –the restaurant opens at half past eight.

Morning, afternoon and night

To express general times of the day use the expressions 'de la mañana', 'de la tarde' and 'de la noche.'

'Son las tres de la tarde' –it's three in the afternoon.

'Es la una de la mañana' –it's one in the morning.

'Son las once de la noche' –it's eleven at night.

Telling the time

To tell the time is 'dar la hora.'

Time Advanced

Speaking about the moment

'El tiempo' means the general idea of time but it also means 'weather', so if you want to say 'let's meet at another time' you have to say 'quedemos otro día' or 'otra ocasión,' otherwise you may confuse the listener.

More right now expressions

'No es el momento adecuado' – it's not the right moment.

'Llegar el momento' – the moment has arrived.

'Por ahora' – for now.

'En seguida' – immediately.

'A este ritmo...' – at this rate...

If you wish to say 'in time,' as in 'in time he will learn' it is 'con el tiempo'.

'In time' (as in within the period of time) is 'a tiempo' while 'on time' (as in to be punctual) is 'puntual'.

Periods of time

A period of time in the past in Spanish is called an 'época.' This can mean a century, decade, or even week in both the recent and distant past. It is therefore common to hear 'en esa época estudiaba francés' – at that time he was studying French.

If you wish to say something happened around that time (but you're not sure when exactly) then you use the preposition 'por.' For example, 'fue por los años cincuenta' – it was around the 50s.

A little while in past and future
If you want to say something happened only a little while ago you say 'pasó hace poco'. If you want to say something will happen in a short while then it you say 'pasará dentro de poco'. Another option for future is 'en un rato' ('rato' meaning 'awhile.')

Speaking in the long and short term
'In the long term' in Spanish is 'a largo plazo' while 'in the short term' is 'a corto plazo.' For example:
'A corto plazo las acciones bajarán pero a largo plazo el valor aumentará' – in the short term the shares will go down but in the long term their value will increase.
Another way to say 'in the long term' is 'a la larga.'

More useful long and short term expressions
'Temporal' – temporary.
'Permanente' – permanent.
'Aplazar y posponer'– to put off or postpone.
'Ante ayer' – the day before yesterday.
'Pasado mañana' –the day after tomorrow.

Lateness/earliness
If you're running late you never say 'estoy tarde' instead you say 'llego tarde' ('I arrive late') and if you're early 'llego temprano.'
Once you've arrived you say, 'perdona por el retraso' ('Sorry for my lateness') for whoever has been waiting for you.

33. The weather

Weather is expressed with the verb **hacer + adjective or noun** and so instead of saying 'it is cold today' you are actually saying 'it makes cold today.'

Weather expressions with 'hacer'

Questions

You have a few options for 'what's the weather like?' these are: '¿Qué tiempo hace?' and '¿Qué clima hace?' or ¿Cómo está el tiempo hoy? (how is the weather today?)

Answers

'Hace frío' – it's cold.

'Hace calor' – it's hot.

'Hace viento' – it's windy.

'Hace sol' – it's sunny.

'Hace buen tiempo esta semana' – the weather is good this week.

'Hacía mal tiempo la semana pasada' – the weather was bad last week.

Expressing degrees

To express degree add 'mucho', 'bastante' or 'un poco.' For example:

'Hace mucho frío hoy' – it's very cold today.

'Hacía bastante sol ayer' – it was quite sunny yesterday.

Expressions with 'estar'

If you want to say something is happening now, use **estar + verb in gerund**. Estar is also used for a few adjectives. For example:

Answers

'Está oscuro' – it's dark.

'Está nublado' –it's cloudy.

'Está lloviendo' –it's raining.

'Está nevando' – it's snowing.

Expressions with 'hay'

Hay + adjective or noun also expresses weather. For example:

'Hay niebla' – it's foggy.

'Hay sol' – the sun is shining.

'Hay luna' – the moon is out.

'Hay relámpagos' – it's lightning.

'Hay humedad' – it's humid.

'Hay nubes' – it's cloudy.

'Hay lluvias torrenciales' – it's pouring.

'Hay un vendaval' –there's a gale.

'Hay granizo' – it's hailing.

'Hay tormenta' – there is a storm.

34. Measuring length and depth

Measurements often cause problems for English speakers as you cannot use 'how + adjective' for your questions. For measurements such as 'how long, tall, wide', you instead use **cuánto** + **medir** ('to measure'). For example:

'¿Cuánto mide tu hermano?' – how tall is your brother? (or literally 'how much does your brother measure?)

'Mi hermano mide metro 85' – My brother is one meter 85 cms tall.

If you need to be more specific and ask the width of something (rather than the height) ask:

'¿Cuánto mide la mesa de ancho?' – how wide is the table? (or literally 'how much does the table measure of wide?)

To talk about weight use **cuánto's** + **kilos** + **pesar** (or another measurement of weight) or **cuánto** + **pesar** (to weigh). For example:

'¿Cuántos kilos pesa tu hermano?' – how heavy is your brother? (or literally 'how many kilos does your brother weigh?)

'Pesa 86 kilos' – he weighs 86 kilos.

'¿Cuánto pesa el mundo?' – how much does the world weigh?

Dimensions

Adjective	Noun
largo – long	longitud – length
ancho – wide	anchura – width
profundo – deep	profundidad – depth
alto – tall/ high	altura – height
espeso – thick	densidad – thickness

35. Measuring distance and directions

Distance

The distance question would be either:

A qué distancia está + place one + de + place two

Or

A cuántos + measurement + está + place one + de + place two

For example:

'¿A qué distancia está París de Londres?' – how far is Paris from London?

'¿A cuántos kilómetros está Málaga de aquí?' – how far is Malaga from here?

To talk about distance with a measurement of time it is:

A cuánto tiempo está + place one + de + place two + method of transport

- o   En coche
- o   En tren
- o   En avión
- o   Caminando/a pie (on foot)

For example: '¿A cuánto tiempo está la iglesia de aquí caminando?' – how far is the church from here on foot?

Directions

Asking for directions is an essential language function. The only significant difference between English and Spanish is that 'cerca' ('close') carries the preposition 'de' rather than 'a' ('to'). All places are expressed with 'estar,' as their location changes depending upon where you are.

Questions
- '¿Dónde está...?' – where is (the)...?
- '¿A qué distancia está el hospital de la estación?' – how far is the hospital from the station?
- ¿Cómo llego a ...? – how do I get to...?

Answers
'Está...'
- a la izquierda – to the left.
- a la derecha – to the right.
- recto – straight.
- al lado de – next to.
- delante de – infront of.
- detrás de – behind.
- cerca de – near to.
- lejos de – far from.

More vocabulary
'Sigue todo recto' – keep going straight.
'Girarte' – turn.
'Dar la vuelta' – to do a u-turn.
'Estar en camino de' – to be on your way to.

Road vocabulary
'Atasco' – traffic jam.
'Carriles' – lanes.
'Derecho de paso' – right of way.
'Peatones' – pedestrian.
'Paso de peatones; paso de cebra' – zebra crossing.
'Rotonda' – roundabout.
'Semáforo' – traffic light.

36. Receiving services

The main thing to remember when ordering or buying is that there is no literal equivalent to 'can I have'. Instead you must use the phrase 'puedes darme' – can you give me? or in Spain it is common to hear simply 'dame' (give me). If you wish to be more polite you can use 'me gustaría…' (I would like) or 'le gustaría…' (She or he would like).

Shopping for items

Questions

The most common price question is '¿cuánto vale?' or '¿cuánto valen?' – how much is it or they worth?

Other price questions are:

'¿Cuánto es?' or '¿cuánto son?' – how much is it/ are they?

¿Cuánto cuesta? ¿Cuánto cuestan? — how much does it cost? how much do they cost?

Remember: If the question contains the item you cannot use 'cuánto/a es?' (for example 'cuánto es el pan' is wrong) you must instead use 'cuánto/a cuesta' or 'cuánto/a vale.'

More phrases and verbs

'¿Hay descuento?' – Is there a discount?

'¿Está de rebajas?' – is there a sale on?

'¿Hay garantía?' — Is there a guarantee?

'Busco….' – I am looking for…

'¿Dónde puedo comprar …?' — Where can I buy …?

'Comprar'— to buy.

'Devolver' – to take back.

'Probarse' – to try one.

'Probadores' – changing rooms.

'La caja/ el cajero' — cash register.

'Tíquet' – receipt.

Shopping for food

Prices

When speaking about money when buying food, use 'estar' rather than 'ser' as the price of fruit and vegetables varies by the day. For example:

'Los plátanos están más baratos hoy porque tenemos oferta' – the bananas are cheaper today because we have an offer.

'¿A cuánto está la fruta hoy?' – how much is the fruit today?

When asking about quality also use 'estar' or 'salir'. For example:

'¿Cómo están los tomates hoy?' – how are the tomatoes today?

'¿Qué tal salen las manzanas?' – how are the apples?

Slices

One thing to note when buying things is that there are different words for 'to slice/a slice'. When asking for cake the noun is 'trozo' (verb 'trocear'). When asking for ham and other cold meats the noun is 'lonchas' (verb 'cortar en lonchas'). When asking for bread the noun is 'rebanadas' (verb 'cortar en rebanadas'). For example:

'Dos trozos de tarta, cuatro lonchas de jamón y tres rebanadas de pan por favor' – two slices of cake, four slices of ham and three slices of bread please.'

Explaining that you have run out of something

The verb 'to run out' is 'agotarse' in Spanish. For example:

'Se nos ha agotado la leche' – we have run out of milk (or literally, 'the milk has run out for us').

However, a more common expression in this situation is 'no queda' ('it doesn't remain') and the question in a shop for 'do you still have...?' would be 'queda..?' ('does it remain?'). For example:

'¿Queda pan?' 'no, no queda.'

'To be out of' is **estamos sin + noun**. For example:

'Estamos sin pan desde esta mañana.'

The verb for 'to pass a use-by-date' is 'caducar.'

For example:

'No comas la mantaquilla, ha caducado' – don't eat the butter it has passed its use-by-date.

This verb can also be used for 'to expire.' For example:

'La oferta caduca en mayo' – the offer runs out ('expires') in May.

Dining out

'Menu' in Spanish is 'la carta.' 'El menú' is for a set menu such as 'el menú del día.' If you want to say something was tasty use **estar + adjective** – for example, 'está bueno' ('the food is good') or 'Ésa estaba deliciosa' ('that was delicious'.)

Questions

'¿Cuál es el menú del día?' – what is the set menu today?

'¿Qué está incluido?' – what is included?

'¿Qué me recomienda?' – what do you recommend?

Expressions

'La cuenta, por favor' – the bill, please.

'Quisiera reservar una mesa para dos' – I'd like to reserve a table for two.

Basic vocabulary

'La bebida' – beverage.

'La comida' – food/lunch.

'Entrantes' – starters.

'Plato principal' – main course.

'El postre' – dessert.

'El pimiento' – pepper.

'La sal' – salt.

Having your hair cut

'To have your hair cut' in Spanish is 'cortarse el pelo' even though you're not doing it yourself. For example:

'Mañana mi madre va a cortarse el pelo' – tomorrow my mother is going to have her hair cut.

Other words

'Corte de pelo' – haircut.

Household problems and getting something fixed

Household bills are called 'recibos.' The electricity bill is called 'recibo de la luz,' the water bill, 'el recibo de agua' and so on.

If you're looking for a place to rent it will either come 'amueblado' ('furnish') or 'sin muebles' (unfurnished). If you have a problem you can call 'el propietario' or 'la propietaria' or one of the below trades people.

'El/la carpintero/a' – carpenter.

'El/la electricista' – electrician.

'El/la fontanero/a' – plumber.

'Inmobiliaria' – estate agent.

'Técnico' – technician.

Useful phrases

'Reparar' – to repair/ fix.

'Fregar el suelo' –to mop the floor.

'Hacer la cama' – make the bed.

'Hacer la limpieza' – do the cleaning.

'Lavar los platos' –to wash the dishes.

'Pasar la aspiradora' – do the hoovering.

'Quitar el polvo' – to dust.

'Estar a tope' – it's full to the brim.

At the bank

'To open an account' is 'abrir una cuenta bancaria.' To do this banks typically ask for your 'nómina' (pay slip) or 'un justificante de los ingresos' – evidence of your incoming money. 'To lend' is 'prestar' while 'to borrow' is 'tomar prestado.'

Loan vocabulary

'La deuda' – debt.

'Préstamo' – loan.

'Hipoteca' – mortgage.

'Deber' – to owe.

'Devolver' – to pay back.

'Amortizar' – to pay back a loan.

'Pagar a plazos' – to pay by instalments.

'Ahorrar' –to save up.

More expressions

'Permitirse' –to afford.

'El plus' – bonus.

'Estar sin blanca' – to be broke.

'Llevar a la quiebra' – to go bankrupt.

'Heredar' – to inherit.

'Herencia' – inheritance.

'La paga' – pocket money.

'Subida de sueldo' – payrise.

'Las acciones' – shares.

'Accionistas' – shareholders.

37. Chatting with friends

Chatting with people you know well is one of the most rewarding things about learning Spanish. It also means you must learn to use a wide variety of language functions to cover different types of conversation. These I have categorised below.

Meeting friends

If you see a friend in the street, you'd probably say 'qué gusto verte' (how great to see you) or 'cuánto tiempo sin verte' (how long has it been?) or even 'me alegro de verte' (great to see you). This is followed by a '¿cómo estás?', '¿qué tal?' or '¿cómo va todo?' which all mean 'how are you?' or 'how's it going?' If you want to buy them a beer/coffee you would say 'te invito un café' from the verb 'invitar' (I'll buy you a coffee.')

Apologising, thanking and congratulating

'Thank you' is **gracias por + infinitive**. 'To thank' is the verb **agradecer'** + **a + person** or without preposition when followed by a noun. For example: 'Les agradezco las propuestas' – I thank them for the proposals.
To apologise say 'perdón' or 'perdóname' ('forgive me') for actions that are not serious (such as being late) and 'siento' or 'lo siento' for actions that have done more damage (such as breaking someone's favourite teapot).
When speaking about feeling bad about what is happening to someone else (and is not connected to you), use **sentir + que + subjunctive**. For example: 'Siento que tengas estos problemas' – I am sorry that you have these problems. You can also substitute 'sentir' for 'lamentar que' + subjunctive (if speaking of someone else) or + indicative if speaking about yourself.

To ask for forgiveness from someone else say 'te pido perdón' (forgive me) or '¿me perdonas?' with 'perdonar' in subjunctive form.

More phrases
'Gracias aun así' – thanks all the same.
'¿Puedes perdonarme?' – can you forgive me?

Expressing likes and dislikes
You already know the verb 'gustar' but there are many ways to say to like and dislike something. Many of these are 'back to front' verbs like 'gustar' and follow the system:

Indirect object pronoun + verb in third person singular or plural
For example:
'Le gustan las mazanas pero a mí no me gusta la tarta' – he likes apples but I don't like cake.
For the sake of simplicity I will show these verbs with le + verb.
If you want to say someone really likes something you could say 'estar enganchado al/ a la + noun' this means 'to be hooked on.' For example:
'Están enganchado al ajedrez' – they are hooked on chess.
Becareful, however, as just like English it can mean also mean 'to be addicted'.

Phrases for liking something
'Le encanta algo' – she loves something.
'Le apetece algo' – she fancies something.
'Le dan ganas de + infinitive' – she is looking forward to doing something..
'Soy aficionado a' – I am a fan of.
'Le mola' – He likes it (an informal version of 'gustar' often used by young people).
'¡Qué mola! – How cool! (young trendy way).

'¡Qué guay!' – How cool! (normal way).
'Sale de muerte' – it's to die for (food)

Phrases for not liking something

'No le gusta algo' – he doesn't like something.
'No soportar algo' – to can't stand something.
'Odiar algo' – to hate something.
'No soy aficionado a' – I am not a fan of.
'Mis gustos son diferentes' – my tastes are different.
'La película es una mierda/ es una película de mierda' – the film is shit (vulgar).

To like or dislike a person

Expressing a like or dislike for a person is expressed with **le cae bien/mal alguien** (literally, they fall well or badly with me). For example:
'Me caen bien los compañeros de clase' – I like my classmates.
'Le cae mal su maestra' – he doesn't like his teacher.

To get on well (or not) with someone is **Llevarse bien/mal con alguien**. For example:
'Mis hermanos y yo nos llevamos muy bien, pero nos llevamos mal con nuestro primo' – my siblings and I get on very well but we get on badly with our cousin.
While to get very badly is 'se llevan a matar.'
If you are emotionally close to someone use the phrase 'estar unido'.
For example, 'estamos unidas, mis hermanas y yo' – my sisters and I are close.

Talking about ages

When speaking about the age of someone of maturing years, to refer to someone as 'viejo/a' (old) is a borderline insult. Instead someone is 'mayor' which means 'older' but in a more respectful way. 'Mayor' is also used for a comparison in age.

For example:

'Mi hijo es más mayor que mi hija' – my son is older than my daughter.

When speaking about someone young you use the term 'joven' for both sexes or 'jovencito/a.' When speaking in comparisons use the word 'menor.' For example:

'Mi hija es la menor del clase' – my daughter is the youngest in the class.

When speaking about approximations in age, use **tener + unos + años**.

For example, 'tiene unos 50 años – he is around 50.

Questions

You have two standard options for 'how old is someone?. These are:

¿Cuántos años tiene? and ¿Qué edad tiene?

Note: If asking the age of a baby you can also use ¿Cuánto tiempo tiene?

Speaking about a time in someone's life

When speaking about a period of time in someone's life that is now finished use:

Imperfect + de bebé, de pequeño, de adolecente, de joven, de soltero/a, de casado/a and so on. For example:

'Antes vivía en Australia, de pequeño' – I used to live in Australia when I was a child.

'Ella no dormía mucho de bebé – she didn't sleep much as a baby.

'Tocaba la guitarra en una banda de joven' – I used to play guitar in a band when I was young.

Antes de soltera, salía mucho con mis amigas' – When I was single I used to go out a lot.

Speaking about a certain age in someone's life

To speak about an event that happened at an age in someone's life use:

Preterite+ a + los + años. For example:

'Aprendí a conducir a los 18 años' – I learnt to drive at 18.

'Me fui de la casa a los 21 años' – I left home at 21.

Birth and death

Birth is expressed with the regular verb 'nacer' and death with the stem-change verb 'morir' if the death was unnatural and 'morirse' if the death was natural. For example:

'Nací en los ochenta' – I was born in the eighties.

'Mi abuelo se murió a los noventa años' – my grandfather died at 90.

'Mi antepasado murió en la guerra' – my ancestor died in the war.

The action of 'to give birth' is 'dar a luz a alguien' while the noun 'birth' is 'parto'.

For example, 'el parto duró 12 horas' – the birth lasted 12 hours.

Secrets

'To keep a secret' is 'guardar un secreto' while 'to tell a secret' is 'contar un secreto.' However, you 'decir la verdad o una mentira' (to tell the truth or a lie). If the person didn't believe your secret you would say 'te lo juro' ('I swear').

More expressions

'Mantener su palabra' – to keep one's word.

Luck

'To be lucky' is 'tener suerte' when speaking about a situation and 'ser afortunado/a' when speaking about people. For example:

'Mi hija tuvo suerte en su examen, no estudió pero sacó un 8.5' – my daughter was lucky in her exam, she didn't study but got a 8.5.

'Sí, pero es afortunada, tiene dos padres que le apoyan' – yes, but she is lucky, she has two supportive parents.

More luck expressions

'Buena suerte' – good luck. (People, however, ususally just say 'suerte'. For example, 'Suerte con tu nuevo trabajo'.)

'Mala suerte' – bad luck.

'Golpe de suerte' – a stroke of luck.

Sentence fillers

There are many words we use not to communicate anything concrete but rather encourage the conversation along. Spanish has as many of these words as English. Here is a curated list.

'A propósito de Paula' – speaking about Paula.

'De todos modos, de todas maneras…' –anyway…

'Hablamos de todo un poco' – we spoke about this and that.

'Pues nada' – OK, well thanks anyway.

'De nada' – no problem, don't worry about it.

'Y tal' – and so on.

Encouraging and discouraging

Encouraging

The word you use for encouraging depends on the situation. If you're cheering on your daughter's football team you would shout '¡Ánimo!' from the verb 'animarse' meaning 'to energise yourself' 'To motivate' or 'to cheer up.' Likewise, if your friend was flagging while studying you would say 'venga amigo, anímate' ('Come on friend, motivate yourself'). To encourage someone to perform well at something for example a music recital, you say '¡dale caña!' ('Hit it' or 'give it some!).

If you wish to talk about encouraging good practices, the verb you're looking for is 'fomentarse.' For example:
'En esta empresa fomentamos la cooperación entre los departementos' – in this company we encourage cooperation between departments.
If you need to encourage someone to do something that requires strength use 'hacer fuerza' meaning 'with all your force.'
For example, if you're trying to change a tyre and can't get it off the wheel someone may say to you, '¡Venga haz fuerza!'
Finally, 'to energise yourself is 'ponete las pilas'. Literally, to put your batteries in.

Giving and receiving advice

Giving and receiving advice is one of the most common language functions between friends. The most common structure is **aconsejar que + subjunctive**.
For example:
'Te aconsejo que no aceptes el puesto' – I advise you not to accept the position.

Pedir que and rogar que ('to beg that') follow the same system.
To give advice is 'dar consejo,' which is a commonly used alternative to the verb.
You may also say 'si yo fuera tú + conditional' which in English is, 'if I were you, I would...' Spanish speakers often shorten this to 'yo de ti' + conditional.
For example:

'Yo de ti, no aceptaría el puesto' – if I were you, I wouldn't take the position.
'Yo de ella pediría la promoción' – if I were her, I would ask for a promotion.

As advice requires sensitive language most phrases are with **que + subjunctive**. For example:
Puede ser que + subjunctive – it could be that.
Es necesario que + subjunctive (when referring to someone else) + indicative (when referring to you)

When you don't want advice
Someone who sticks their nose in someone else's business is a 'entrometido/a' and so you could say to someone 'no seas entrometido/a' ('don't be nosy'), if someone if prying into your business.
The verb for 'to get involved in other people's business' is 'entrometerse' and so if your friend was getting involved in things that didn't concern them you may say '¡no te entrometas!' or even 'no te metas' which means the same thing.
Another way would be to say 'estás metiendo las narices en cosas que no te interesan' (you are sticking your nose into things that don't concern you).

Asking for favours
To ask for a favour you can 'pedir un favor' or if you know the person well you can say **'Hazme el favor de' + indicative** (Do me a favour)
'Haz' is 'hacer' in imperative form. For the vosotros form this is 'haced el favor de' and for usted 'hagan el favor de.'

Ideas
Useful expressions using the noun 'idea.'
Tengo una idea – I have an idea.

¿Dónde están las llaves? No tengo ni idea – where are the keys? I don't have any idea (or 'I have no clue').

¿De dónde sacas esas ideas? – where do you get these ideas from?

Telling a story

The word story in Spanish is either 'el cuento' or 'la historia.'

If you're telling a story to friends in a café they might tell you to 'comenzar desde el principio' – to start from the beginning.

You would then narrate the story or 'narrar la historia' using reported speech.

If you're telling a story from a book you may start with 'érase una vez había…' (once upon a time there was…).

Telling and receiving a joke

When you can tell a decent joke in Spanish you know that your language skills must be pretty good. To make someone laugh is **darle risa que + subjunctive** (when caused by something else) or + **indicative** (when caused by you or speaking generally).

For example:

'Me da risa cuando dices cosas así' – it makes me laugh when you say things like that.

Another way to say this is 'hacerle reír,' which works with the same system.

'Le hace reír que su jefe no sepa usar el ordenador' – it makes him laugh that his boss doesn't know how to use the computer.

More useful phrases

'Bromear' – to joke.

'Burlón' – big joker.

'¡Chispa!' – jinx!

'¡Ni de broma!' – you're joking!

'Reirse de algo' – to laugh at something.

'Tomar el pelo' – to kid someone.

'Has picado' – you fell for it (joke).

'Menuda broma' – what a joke.

'¡Qué gracia! ¡qué comico! ¡qué divertido!' – how funny!

When you're not in the mood for jokes

'No te hagas el tonto' – don't be silly.

'No estoy para bromas hoy' – I am not in the mood for jokes today.

Organising a date

Organising when and where to do something is also a common language function. 'To meet up' is 'quedar,' as opposed to 'encontrar,' which refers to bumping into someone by accident.

If you want to say something works out well or badly for you it is 'va bien/mal.'

For example:

'Esta fecha no me va bien porque tengo una reunión' – this date doesn't work for me because I have a meeting.

A variation would be 'convenirle bien/mal' which means 'to suit.'

When speaking about working out a problem however, use 'solucionar.'

For example:

'Solucionaremos la fecha otro día' – we'll work out the date another day.

Another useful verb is 'arreglar' meaning 'to sort out' or 'to arrange.'

For example:

'Arreglaremos esto cuando quedemos cara a cara' – we'll sort this out when we meet face to face.

If you've arranged everything and someone wants to make changes at the last moment you could say 'todo está arreglado, no podemos dar marcha atrás ahora' – everything is arranged, we can't go back now.

Other useful phrases

'Cara a cara' – face to face.

'Me encargo yo' – I'll take charge.

'Piénsalo bien' – think it over.

'Eso depende de ti' – it's up to you.

'Vamos a ver' – we'll see.

'A la orden' – as you wish (boss/employee relationship).

Commiserating

The main commiserating phrases are 'vaya tela' or 'qué tela' which both mean 'what a nightmare.' If something terrible has happened you can also say 'cuánto lo siento' which means 'I am so sorry.'

More phrases

'La vida es así' – life is like this.

'No puedes ni imaginarlo' – you can't even imagine.

'Superar' – to overcome something emotionally or physically

Pasar la pagina – to turn the page literally (a book) and figuratively (life).

Expressing difference and similarity

If something is different you say 'es diferente a' or 'es distinto a.' For example:
'La práctica es diferente a la competición' – practicing is different than competitions.

If something is the same you can say **es igual que + indicative** or **es lo mismo que + indicative**. For example:
'Pasar un día en la playa es igual que pasar un día en la piscina' – spending a day at the beach is the same as spending a day by the pool.

If you want to say a comparison with an adjective use **ser + igual + de + adjective**.

For example:

'Eres igual de alto que mi hermano' – you are the same height as my brother.

Equally you can use **ser + tan + adjective + como**. 'Eres tan alto como mi hermano.'

More similarity expressions

'Es parecido a' – it's similar to.

'Es similar a' – it's similar to.

'Coincidir' – to coincide.

'Justo como' – just like.

'Me da igual' – it's the same to me or I don't care/mind (literally 'it gives me the same').

Talking about an end

I mention this because there are many ways to express an end to something in Spanish, all meaning something different.

To finish doing something is 'terminar de hacer algo' or 'acabar de hacer algo.'

To put an end to something is **terminar con + noun**. For example:

'Terminó con las quejas' – she put an end to the complaints.

'To end up' (as in you had a plan but ended up doing something else) is **acabar + gerund.** For example:

'Hice una tarta para él pero acabé comiéndola yo mismo' – I made a cake for him but I ended up eating it myself.

'Finally' is usually 'al final,' when speaking about a sequence of events. For example:

'Al final decidimos ir al cine' – finally we decided to go to the cinema.

If you're speaking about something that has finally happened after a lot of waiting, however, you would use '¡por fin!'

For example, '¡Por fin ha salido el sol!' – finally, the sun has come out!

And to finish there is **total que + indicative**. This is an informal way to say that I've decided I'm going to do this and I am not going to change my mind. For example:

'Estoy cansado, total que no voy a la fiesta' – I am tired and so finally I am not going the party.

Saying that someone looks familiar

If someone or something looks familiar use the phrase 'sonarle.' For example:

'Tu jefa me suena' – your boss looks familiar to me.

'Sonarle' is a very common phrase and is used for names, places and ideas much in the same way as we use 'to ring a bell' in English.

More examples:

'¿Conoces el pueblo Moraira?', 'no, pero me suena' – do you know the town Moraira? No but it rings a bell.

38. Appearance and personality

Talking about appearance

There are many verbs used to describe appearance. The most common of these is 'parecerse' ('to seem like') which is used when making comparisons between two people. For example:

'Mis hijos se parecen' – my children look alike

'¿A quién te pareces en tu familia?' – who do you look like in your family?

'Pues, me parezco a mi madre de aspecto y a mi padre de personalidad' – well I look like my mother but I am like my father.

If you're walking down the street and you see someone who to you looks like a bad sort you would say 'tiene mal pinta' and to a lesser extent if you saw someone very beautiful you would say 'tiene buen pinta.'

If you wish to say that someone is looking good (as in 'hot') today you would use **estar** + **bueno/a**. Likewise if you wish to say that someone appears young, (rather than is young) you would say, 'está joven tu abuela.'

Another way to say the above would be, 'se ve bien para su edad, tu abuelo' – your grandfather looks well for his age.

The questions for what do you look like are:

'¿Qué aspecto tiene?' Or '¿Cómo es él/ella ?'

If the listener requires more clarification you can say '¿Cómo es él físicamente?'

While 'who do you look like?' (as in 'who do you resemble?) would be: '¿A quién te pareces?'

Appearance from day-to-day

If you want to talk about your day to day appearance then use the verb 'verse', which means 'I look good' or 'verle' to mean 'you look good.' For example:

'¿Cómo me veo?' – how do I look?

'Te veo muy bien' – you look good.

'Le veía muy bien cuando la encontré' – She was looking very well when I met her.

Short and tall

To say that someone is tall is 'ser alto/a' while to say someone is short is 'ser bajo/a' (or literally 'to be low').

Appearance in clothes

If you want to say if something does or doesn't suit you it is **quedarle bien/mal**.

For example:

'Los vaqueros no me quedan bien' – the jeans don't suit me.

'Te queda bien'– it suits you.

If you want to say that something is tight, loose, long or short on you use:

Quedarle + estrecho, ancho, largo, corto

Hair styles and facial hair

Hair styles and facial hair are expressed with **llevar + style/cut.** For example:

'Lleva fleqillo y pelo largo' – she has a fringe and long hair.

'Lleva barba, bigote y patillas' – he has a beard, a moustache and sideburns.

Hair: Liso (straight), rizado (curly), ondulado (wavy), canas (grey), rubio/a (blond), castaño/a (brunette) pelirojo/a (redhead), calvo/a (bald).

Beard: barba (beard), bigote (moustache), sin barba (clean-shaven).

To lose weight and to gain weight

To express weight loss use the verb 'adelgarzarse' ('to lose weight') and the adjective 'delgado/a'. For example:

'Te veo muy delgada ¿Te has adelgazado?' – you look very slim, have you lost weight?

Equally you could use 'ponerse en forma' ('to get into shape') or 'perder peso' ('to lose weight').

To express weight gain use 'engordarse' ('to gain weight/get fat'). Just as in English though, proceed with caution, as the phrase '¿te has engordado?' doesn't go down well in either language.

Another option is 'ganarpeso' ('to put on weight') and a polite way to refer to a heavy person is 'tener sobrepeso' or ('to be overweight') or 'tener barriga' ('to have a belly').

Talking about personality

For descriptions of someone's personality use **ser + adjective**, unless the characteristic is impermanent, in which case you use **estar + de + adjective**. For example:

'Mi padre es trabajador pero hoy está perezoso' – my father is a hardworker but today he is (feeling) lazy.

Estar + personality adjective often expresses sarcasm or irony. For example in the phrase 'estás generoso hoy' means 'oh so you're being generous *today*.'

Positive personality traits

Encantador (charming), simpático/a (kind), valiente (brave), relajado/a (easy-going), gracioso/comico (funny) maduro/a (mature), alegre (cheerful), agudo (whitty), sabio (wise), hablador/a (talkative), pensativo (thoughtful), empollón (swot), fiel (loyal), inteligente (smart), comprensivo (understanding), trabajador (hardworking), delicado (delicate/graceful).

Negative personality traits

Mandón/a (bossy), celoso/a (jealous), egoista (selfish), sensible (sensitive), cabezón/cabezota (stubborn), olvidadizo (forgetful), descuidado (careless), perezoso (lazy), aprovechado (an opportunist), torpe (clumsy).

Questions

The question for personality is '¿Cómo es él/ella?' or '¿Cómo es de personalidad?'

'¿Cómo es?' is the blanket description for what something or someone is permanently like. If you want to ask 'how are you today' it is of course, '¿cómo estás?'

More examples:

'¿Cómo era tu abuelo?' – what was your grandfather like?

'¿Cómo es tu trabajo?' – what is your work like?

'Tender a' is the stem-change verb meaning to tend to do something and the noun is 'tendencia' ('tendency'). 'Tender a' conjugates like 'tener.' For example:

'Tiendo a leer por las noches' – I tend to read at night.

'La gente tiene tendencia a creer a los periódicos' – people tend to believe the newspapers.

The senses

The senses are as follows. All of these verbs apart from 'tocar' are irregular – the strangest one being 'oler' which is conjugated 'huelo', 'huelas,' 'huela', 'olemos', 'oléis', 'huelen'.

oler – to smell	el olor - smell
sonar – to sound/ring	el sonido - sound
saber – to taste	el sabor - taste
tocar – to touch	el tacto - touch
ver – to see	la vista – sight

Questions

Questions are composed with **a** + **qué** + **verb**.

'¿A qué huele? Huela a rosa' – What does it smell like? It smells like roses.

'¿A qué suena? Suena al autobús' – What does it sound like? It sounds like the bus.

'¿A qué sabe? Sabe a chocolate' – What does it taste like? It tastes like chocolate.

'¿A qué se siente? Siente a lana' – What does it feel like? It feels like wool.

'¿Cómo es físicamente? Se parece a una pelota' – What does it look like? It looks like a ball.

39. Talking about feelings and physical states

To express how someone is feeling use **estar + adjective** as it is an impermanent state. For example:

'Estoy aburrido con esta película y ella está cansada' – I am bored with this film and she is tired.

The object provoking the feeling, however, is expressed with 'ser' and adjective, which usually (though not excusively) ends in 'ante.' For example:

'Estoy preocupada porque los exámenes son preocupantes' – I am worried because the exams are worrying.

To express the process of getting bored or tired then use the reflexive verbs 'aburrirse' and 'cansarse'. More about this in the Become Verbs chapter here.

If you wish to say something about someone's mood or appearance that day then use:

Parecer + adjective

For example:

'Parecen estresados hoy' – they look stressed today.

'Pareces enfadado conmigo' – you seem angry with me.

How to express
Tiredness

A common way to express tiredness is to say 'tengo sueño' as 'sueño' means sleep as well as dream. If you haven't had enough sleep you are suffering from 'falta de sueño' and if something makes you sleepy, such as some medicine, you would say 'la pastilla me da sueño.'

If you got a bad night's sleep you would say 'anoche pasé un noche de perros' (literally, 'last night I passed a night of the dogs'). Another way to say this would be 'he pasado la noche en vela' (literally, I spent the night by candle).

Finally, if you're at a birthday party and your child starts screaming because they're tired you would say to the host, 'perdona, no puede más' – I'm sorry she can't carry on anymore.

Excitement and happiness

'Emocionarse de' is not a perfect translation in English. It is both positive and negative and it means both 'to get excited about' and 'to be emotional about.' In Spanish 'how exciting' would be 'qué emocionante' while expressing your excitement about something would be 'estoy emocionada de +infinitive.'

Another way express excitement is to say you're looking forward to something. In Spanish, this is **tener ganas de + infinitive** or hacer **ilusion que + infinitive.**

For example:

'Mi hermano tiene ganas de terminar el curso' – my brother is looking forward to finishing his course.

If you've just found out you've passed your exams with flying colours you 'saltar de alegría' (jump for joy) and if it's a really hot day and you jump into a cool river you say '¡qué gusto!' (what joy!). To say something is exciting is 'ser ilusionante.'

Awkwardness and embarrassment

Let's say you have a neighbour who suddenly stops speaking to you and when she sees you in the hallway she slams the door of her apartment. In Spanish, she would be described as 'extraño/a' (from the verb extrañarse) or 'raro/a', both meaning 'strange'.

If your bad neighbour suddenly asked you for money you would describe the situation as 'ser inoportuno' or 'violenta' which both mean 'inappropriate' or 'awkward'. 'Ser violento' also means 'to be violent,' and so your listeners will understand what you mean from the context.

If you are embarrassed by something you say 'tengo vergüenza' or 'qué verguenza,' which literally means you have shame. To a lesser extent 'es embarazoso' could also be used but as 'embarazarse' also means to be pregnant, it is safer to use 'vergüenza.'

Fear

The general way to say you're scared is **tener miedo a + infinitive**. For example:

'Mi marido tiene mierdo a volar' – my husband is scared of flying.

If something scares you, however, you would say 'me da miedo' (it's scary).

If someone gives you a sudden fright by jumping out at you in the street you would say 'Qué susto' (what a fright).

Finally 'to scare away' is 'espantar' and 'to get scared away' is 'espantarse'. For example:

'Los perros espantan las palomas, y las palomas se están espantando' – the dogs are scaring away the pigeons and the pigeons are getting scared.

Other expressions

'Estar muerto/a de mierdo' – to be scared stiff.

Anger or annoyance

There are many ways to express anger or annoyance. The most common way is **me da rabia + indicative**, if you're speaking about something you do or + que + subjunctive when speaking about something someone else does. The rough translation is 'it makes me mad' – though it is used so often it can also mean 'it annoys me.'

For example:

'Me da rabia cuando mi hijo pierda los zapatos ' – it annoys me when my son loses his shoes.

Another way to say the above would be 'me molesta' or 'me fastidia' (it bothers me). Both follow the same pattern as 'me da rabia' and are subjunctive when speaking about someone else. For example:

'Me molesta cuando hagas eso' – it annoys me when you do this.

How annoying would be 'iqué fastidio!' while to lose one's mind is 'perder la razón.'

If you want to say you're angry, use the reflexive verb 'enfadarse con.'

'Me enfado con eso' – I get angry about that.

If you want to downgrade the emotion to being upset then use **darle pena** + **indiciative** (if speaking about something you do) or + que + subjunctive (if speaking about something someone else does). For example:

'Me da pena que la gente sufra tanto' –it upsets me that people suffer so much.

Other expressions

'¿Y a mi qué?' – what's that to me or so what?

'Tener un día de perros' – to have a terrible day

'Estar negro/a' – to be angry

'Buscar un show' – To make a scene

'Plantar cara a alguien' – to stand up to someone.

'Enfrentar a algo' – to confront/face up to something.

Expressions with 'demonios'

'Demonios' basically means 'like hell.' Add it for conversations with friends to make your sentences more colourful.

Examples:

'¿Qué demonios ha pasado?' – what the hell has happened?

'¿Cómo demonios lo has hecho?' – how the hell have you done this?

'Huele a demonios' – it smells like hell.

'Sabe a demonios' – it tastes like hell.

'Es el mismo demonio' – he is a very bad person.

Worry

To be worried about something is 'estar preocupado,' while to say that something is worrying is 'Ser preocupante' or 'ser inquietante.' The verb 'to worry about' is 'preocuparse por.'

Stress

The verb 'to get stressed about' is 'estresarse por.' To be stressed is 'estar estresado' while to say something is stressful is 'ser estresante.'

If you wish to say that something is too much for you right now (as in 'overwhelming') then the verb is 'agobiar' or 'abrumar'. For example:

'La presión de este proyecto me agobia' – the pressure of this project overwhelms me.

A common expression in Spanish is 'no te agobies' which means 'don't stress yourself out,' or 'don't worry about it.'

If something makes you nervous then it is 'ponerle nervioso/a.' For example:

'Volar me pone nervioso' – flying makes me nervous.

If you want to say you can't take something anymore it's 'no puedo más' and for work 'estoy a tope.'

Disappointment

'To disappoint' or 'to let down' is expressed with the verb 'decepcionar'. 'To be disappointed' is 'estar decepcionado' and 'to be disappointing' is 'ser decepcionante.'

If something is a shame, it is 'ser una pena' or 'ser una lastima.' 'Estar desconsolado' means 'to be inconsolable.'

Bravery and cowardliness

There are two ways to say someone is brave in Spanish. You can say that someone 'tiene valor' or 'es valiente.' If someone shows bravery, you say '¡qué valiente!' – how brave!

'Atreverse' means 'to dare'. For example:

'¿Te atreves a tirarte a la piscina?' – do you dare to jump in the swimming pool?

'Ser atrevido' means 'to be a daring person' and is commonly used.

There is also 'no tienes los huevos' ('you don't have the balls') for more colloquial situations.

On the other side 'ser un corbade' means 'to be a coward' and 'ser un gallina' means exactly the same in English – to be a chicken.

Shock

If someone hears incredible news you'll often hear the phrase '¡No me lo puedo creer!' (I can't believe it!) or '¡No me digas!' (You don't say!)

The closest verb for 'to shock' is 'impactarle.' For example:

'No impactó mucho el resulto de las elecciones' – we were shocked about the election.

The word 'shock' has also been incorporated into Spanish and so it is common to hear '¡estoy en shock!' when someone hears bad or surprising news.

Likewise, the phrase 'Oh my God' has been incorporated and is commonly used among young people. The Spanish equivalent is '¡Ay dios mío!' but you must be careful, of course, about using it in front of religious people.

The verb 'impresionar' can be construed as a false friend as it means 'to make an impression on' more than 'to impress' and can be used to express both positive and negative feelings. For example:

'Me impresionó que se presentara al gobierno otra vez' could mean that 'I was impressed that he was running for government again or 'I was shocked that he was running for government again'.

To express your opinion about what someone else does use **qué increíble que + subjunctive**. To express an opinion on something you do use **qué increíble que + indicative**.

Finally, when talking about something that does not shock you but you find slightly strange use the verb 'chocarse' (to crash). For example, if speaking about living in another country you may comment 'me choca que el horario de comer sea diferente' – it's strange to me that the timetable for meals is different.

Surprise

This expressed with the verb 'soprenderle' + subjunctive (when commenting about other events/people) and + indicative (when speaking about you or generally).

For example: 'Me sorprende que no haya conseguido la promoción' – it surprises me (or I am surprised) that she didn't get the promotion.

Other useful phrases

'Marvillarse' – to wonder at.
'Fantástico/genial' – fantastic/ great
'¡Qué bien!' – great!
'¡Fenomenal!' – fantastic!

To mind/ to matter

If you see someone crying in the street you would say '¿qué te pasa?' – what's the matter? The indirect object pronoun is essential here as without it ('¿qué pasa?') you are saying 'what happened?'

'To mind' as in 'to care' is the verb **importarle + que + subjunctive** (when referring to the actions of someone else) and + indicative (when refering to you).

For example: 'No me importa que digan eso' – I don't care if they say that.
'No me importa trabajar esta tarde' – I don't mind working this afternoon.
If someone gave you the option of working on Monday or Tuesday you may say to them 'me da igual' which is a commonly used expression that says you don't care about a choice.

Love and closeness

'To love' is the verb 'querer' or 'amar.'
To go out with someone is 'salir con alguien' while to dump someone is 'dejar a alguien.'
To express closeness to someone is 'estar unido/a.' For example:

'¿No estás unida a tu familia?' 'Estoy unido a mi hermano pero a mis padres, no' – you are not close to your family? I am close to my brother but not to my parents.

To miss someone is 'le/la echar de menos'. For example:'La echo de menos mucho mi hermana' – I miss my sister a lot.

Expressions with darle

Another way to say something provokes a reaction in you is indirect **object pronoun + dar + noun**.

Common phrases:

Darle rabia – to make a person angry.

'Las colas largas me dan rabia' – long queues make me angry.

Darle vergüenza – to make a person embaressed/ashamed.

'La basura en la calle le da mucho vergüenza' – Rubbish in the streets makes him very ashamed.

Darle pena – to make a person pity/upset.

'Le da pena cuando su hijo no saqua buenas notas' – it upsets her when her son doesn't get good marks.

More phrases

'Darle risa' – to make a person laugh.

'Darle miedo' – to make a person scared.

'Darle susto' – to give a person a sudden fright.

'Darle asco' – to disgust someone.

'Darle sueño' – to make a person sleepy.

'Darle estrés' – to make a person stressed.

'Darle calor/frío' – to make a person hot or cold.

'Darle hambre/sed' – to make a person hungry or thirsty.

'Darle ganas de hacer algo' – to make a person want to do something.

'Darle luz' – to cause someone to be blinded by light.

'Darle gusto' – to be pleased by something.

Physical states

Injuries

To hurt as in my arm hurts is **body part + indirect personal pronoun + doler (to hurt).**

'El brazo me duele' – my arm hurts (or literally 'my arm hurts me').

'Los pies me duelen' – my feet hurt (or literally 'My feet hurt me').

For this reason 'doler' like 'gustar' and 'importar' only exists in the third person singular or plural. In addition, it is only used in the present or imperfect form for past.

Its conjugations run:

Present: duele, duelen and **past:** dolía, dolian

If you wish to say 'I hurt my arm' (as in I or something else caused the action), then it is with the verb dañarse (to damage oneself) with the structure **indirect personal pronoun + danarse + en + body part.**

For example, the sentence above would be: 'me he hecho daño en el abrazo'.

More examples:

'Se hizo daño en la muñeca cuando se cayó' – he hurt his wrist when he fell.

'¿Te has hecho daño?' – have you hurt yourself?

'Deja de hacer eso o vas a hacerte daño' – stop doing that or you're going to hurt yourself.

More verbs

'Desangrar' – to bleed.

'Marcarse' – to bruise (moratón – a bruise).

'Quemar' – to burn.

'Una revisión' – a check up.

'Curarse' – to heal/to cure.

'Vacunarse' – to vaccinate (vacuna – vaccine).

'Ponerse una vacuna' – to give a vaccine.

'Tirita' – plasters/bandaid.

'Escayolar' – to put in plaster.

'Operar a alguien' – to operate on someone.

'Recetar' – to prescribe (prescription, receta).

'Dejar un cicatriz' – to scar.

'Puntos' – stitches

'Torcerse' – to twist

'Resultar herido' – to get wounded/injured

'Herida' – wound

Illnesses

To be sick in Spanish is 'estar mailta' while 'to feel sick' is 'encontrarse enfermo' and 'to get sick' 'ponerse enfermo.'

For example:'Mi marido se encuentra enfermo, se puse enfermo ayer después de comer algo malo' – my husband is feeling sick, he got sick yesterday after eating something bad.

There is no word for 'ache' in Spanish. Instead you use:

Tener dolor de + part of the body

For example:'Tengo dolor de cabeza' – I have a headache.

A cold is a 'resfriado' or 'un constipado,' while to catch a cold is 'coger un resfriado.'

To be off from work or school sick is 'estar de baja por enfermedad.' For example:

'Mis hijos estuvieron de baja por enfermedad la semana pasada porque tenian la varicela' – my children were off sick last week because they had chicken pox.

40. Body positions and movements

Body positions

Body positions are not made with a verb as they are in English, but rather **estar de** or **quedarse + noun**. For example: 'To be standing up' is 'estar de pie' or 'quedarse de pie.' To be kneeling is 'estar de rodillas.'

More phrases
- Estar de/quedarse
- Pie – to be standing.
- Perfil – to be in profile.
- Frente – to be standing with your front towards someone.
- Espaldas – to be standing with your back towards someone.
- Rodillas – to be kneeling.

Estar/quedarse
- sentado – to be sitting.
- tumbado – to be lying down.
- doblado – to be bending down.

Body movements

Movement is expressed with **ponerse de + noun.** For example, 'ponerse de pie' – stand up and 'ponerse de rodillas' – kneel down.

More phrases
Ponerse de
- pie – stand up.
- rodillas – kneel down.
- frente – turn yourself to the front.
- perfil – turn yourself to the side.
- espalda – turn yourself to the back.

Expressions with 'dar'

Dar + noun can also be used for a variety of body actions.

Dar
- una torta – a slap.
- un puñetazo – a punch.
- una patada – a kick.
- caña – to spank.
- besos – to kiss.
- darse de narices – to fall flat on your face.
- la espalda - to turn one's back.
- gritos - to shout.
- un abrazo - to embrace, to hug.
- a luz – to give birth.

More expressions

'Bostezar' – to yawn.
'Chillar a alguien' – to scream at.
'Dar la mano' – to shake hands.
'Escupir' – to spit.
'Estornudar' – to sneeze.
'Fruncir el ceño' – to frown.
'Gritar a alguien' – to shout at.
'Guñir' – to wink.
'Roncar' – to snore.
'Señalar' – to point at.
'Saludar' – to wave (hello).
'Susurrar' – to whisper.

To stop

There are several verbs for 'to stop' in Spanish. If something physically stops use the verb 'parar.' For example, 'el tren para en la estación.' If you wish to stop doing something as in 'to give up' the verb is 'dejar de'. For example:

'He dejado de fumar' – I have given up smoking.

You can also say 'dejar de hacer eso' – stop doing that.

If you want to prevent something then the verb is **impedir que + subjunctive**. For example, 'no puedes impedirme que salga con mis amigas' – you can't stop me going out with my friends.

If you stop someone moving, as in 'to detain,' then the verb is 'detener.' For example:

'La policia detuvo al criminal' – The police stopped the criminal.

Finally to give up on your education (as in 'to drop out') or job is 'abandonar.' For example:

'Mis amigos abandonaron los estudios y formaron una banda' – my friends dropped out of their studies and formed a band.

41. Forming an argument

Opinions

In Spanish you use the verb **creer** (to believe) + **que** + **indicative**, rather than 'pensar' (to think), as pensar refers more to the cognitive process than ideas.

Other useful phrases include:

'Para mí' – in my opinion.

'En mi opinión' – in my opinion.

'Opino que' (from the verb 'opinar')– I think that.

To ask someone else's opinion you use **qué** + **indirect object pronoun** + **parecer**. For example:

'¿Qué te parece la película? – what do you think of the film?

Other variations include:

¿Qué opinas? – what do you think?

Pedir la opinión a alguien – to ask somebody's opinión.

Opinions when you don't really know what's happening

'Dicen que' + indicative – They say that.

'Por lo visto' – from the look of things.

'Según dicen' – according to what they say.

'Para algunos' – for some.

'Según la gente' + indicative – according to the people.

Agreeing/disagreeing

This is made using **estar** + **de acuerdo**. It is literally 'I am in agreement'. For example:

'No estoy de acuerdo con el impuesto nuevo' – I don't agree with the new tax.

More phrases

'Tienes razón' – you're right.

'Nos ponemos de acuerdo' – to come to an agreement.

Connectors: And, but and conssequently

Sentence connectors are made by adding one more point ('and'), opposing the last point ('but'), and presenting a consequence.

And

This is largely expressed by 'además de,' which means 'in addition to', 'as well as' and 'besides that'. For example:

'Además de hacer los deberes tienen que practicar la flauta' – as well as doing their homework they have to practice the flute.

Another popular 'and' comes in the form of 'también', which means 'also.'

But

The formal version of 'pero' (but) is **sin embargo + indicative,** which means 'however'.

Other useful phrases include:

'No obstante' + indicative – nevertheless.

'A pesar de (que)' + indicative – despite, in spite of.

'Aunque' + indicative - Although/even though.

'Aunque' + subjunctive - even if.

For more on 'aunque' take a look at the Subjunctive In Past chapter.

Explaining your reasons

The first word you learnt for this was probably 'porque' (because) – however, it is more common to hear 'es que' (it's that). For example:

'Es que estuve cansado ayer, así que no ordené mi cuarto' – it's that I was tired yesterday so I didn't tidy my room.

Another popular phrase is 'por' or 'por eso', which is a shortened version of 'porque.'

For example:

'No podemos preparar la barbacoa por la lluvia' – we can't prepare the barbeque because of the rain.

More reason phrases

'Por el motive que' + indicative – it's for the reason that.
'Lo que pasó es que' + indicative – what happened is that.
'Es por eso que' + indicative – it's for that reason that.
'El caso es que' + indicative – the reason is that.

Note: The word 'razón' (reason) is rarely used when referring to a motive.

More cause and effect phrases:

'A causa de que' + indicative – because of.
'Debido a' + noun – due to.
'Debido a que' + indicative– due to the fact that.
'Puesto que' + indicative – since, as.
'Gracias a (que)' + indicative – thanks to.
'Por culpa (de)' + indicative– because of.
'Por lo tanto' + indicative – therefore.
'Al contrario' – it's the opposite.
'A cambio de que' + subjunctive – in return for.
'Por si' + indicative – in case.
'Me llevo un paraguas por si llueve' – I will take an umbrela in case it rains.

'En consecuencia' – in consequence.

More 'so' options

Special attention must be made to 'so' phrases. 'So' as a vague consequence of a (possibly) unintentional action is **así que** + **indicative.** For example:
'No tengo el número de teléfono así que le enviaré una carta' – I don't have the phone number so I will send a letter.
'So that' which is a definite consequence of an intended action is **para que** + **subjunctive.** For example:
'Lleva un paraguas para que no te mojes' – take an umbrella so that you don't get wet.
Another major consequence word is **entonces** + **indicative** which means 'then' but is often used for 'so'. For example:
'Trabajo mañana, entonces no salgo esta noche' – I am working tomorrow, so I am not going out tonight.'

So far

While we're on 'so' let's take a moment to explore 'so far.' In Spanish this is 'hasta ahora' or if you're speaking about the amount of kilometres driven, potatos peeled or pages read, **llevar** + **participle in plural**. For example:
'Llevo tres páginas leídas' – I have read three pages so far.

Why not

'Why' is 'por qué' + indicative and 'why not' 'por qué' + subjunctive. There is another 'why not', however, used for questions, in the form of '¿cómo que no?' 'Cómo que no?' is used as an incredulous reply when you expected the answer to be yes. It is not usually followed by a verb but when it does it is in indicative. For example:
Pablo: 'Maria, no puedo decirte el secreto. Maria: '¿Cómo que no?'
A variation would be '¿Cómo que nunca?' (why do you never). For example, '¿Cómo que nunca haces ejercicio?' – why do you never do any exercise?

Giving examples

Examples are expressed with 'Por ejemplo' (for example) or to distinguish between several things in a group, 'en particular' (in particular). Another commonly used expression is 'en concreto,' which means 'especially.' 'Especialmente', however, isn't commonly used.

Another difference between English and Spanish is that you say 'ponme un ejemplo' – 'to put me an example' rather than 'to give me an example.'

Structuring your arguments

There are many ways to structure a written argument such as 'primero', 'segundo', 'al final' and so on. Orally, however, people use 'por un lado' (on the one hand) and 'por otro lado' (on the other hand). A variation on this is 'por una parte' and 'por otra parte.'

The way you do something

'De modo que', 'de manera que'and 'de forma que' all explain the way in which the subject does something. If the sentence speaks about the way the subject does something for themselves it is indicative after 'que', if it speaks about the way the subject does something for others, it is subjunctive. For example:

'Lo expliqué muy claro de modo que todos pudieran entenderlo' – I explained it in a way everyone could understand.

'Haz el trabajo de forma que todo salga bien' – do your work in a way that everything works out well.

'Cocino de un modo que es muy creativo' – I cook in a way that is very creative.

The method that you use to do something

To express a method, use 'a medida que' with the same indicative and subjunctive rules as above. For example:

'A medida que estudias, aprendes más' – through the method that you study, you learn more.

'A medida que corras, te pondrás en forma más rapido' – through the way that you run, you will get fit quicker.

Referencing a source

The easiest way to reference a source is with 'según' (according to). For example, 'según el periódico habrá elecciones el año que viene' – according to the newspaper there will be an election next year.

Other useful phrases include:

'En cuanto a' – with respect to, regarding, concerning.

'En relación con' – in relation to.

'Por ejemplo' – for example.

'De hecho' – in fact.

'A saber' – namely.

'Dar por hecho' – take it as read/for granted.

Starting from a fact

These expressions are very similar in English and Spanish and used when starting your sentence from a certain premise or view point.

'Puesto que' –put that way.

'Dado que' – given that.

Uncertainty

Not knowing something is more commonly expressed with 'no tener claro' rather than 'no estar seguro.' For example:

'No tiene claro qué materia tiene que estudiar' – he is not sure which subject he needs to study.

To ask someone if they are sure about something you say '¿Seguro?' rather than '¿Estás seguro?' and the reply would be 'sí, seguro.'

Useful phrases include:

'No lo tengo claro' – I am not sure.

'No sé' – I don't know.

'Supuestamente' – supposedly.

'No estoy seguro' – I am not sure.

'Matiz' – nuance.

'Eso depende de' – it depends on.

'Tener en cuenta' – to take into account.

'Sea como sea' – be that as it may.

'No es cierto' – it's not true.

Certainty and clarifying

Certainty is expressed with 'tener claro' or less commonly 'estoy seguro/a'. A common phrase is also 'Saber a ciencia cierta + indicative' – tto know something for sure.

For example:'Sé a ciencia cierta que me llamarán' – I know for sure that they will call me.

More phrases

'¿En qué sentido?' – in what sense?

Judging an event

Judging an event involves the verb **ser** + **adjective/noun** + **indicative** (when speaking about yourself) or + **que** + **subjunctive** (when speaking about someone else).

Phrases that follow this pattern include:

Ser...

Raro, bueno, malo, sano, inútil, justo, injusto, fácil, difícil, probable, improbable, necesario, importante, suficiente, insuficiente, una tontería, una locura, una pena, una lástima, un placer, una vergüenza, una maravilla, una suerte.

For example:

'Es una suerte que puedas quedarte esta noche' – it's lucky you can stay tonight.

Conclusions

There are as many ways to conclude in Spanish as there are in English.

Useful phrases include:

'Para resumir' – to summarise.

'Para finalizar' – to conclude.

'En pocas palabras' – in short.

'En resumen' – in summary.

'En definitiva' – in brief.

'Por mi parte' – as far as I am concerned.

Confirmations

These phrases confirm either what you're trying to say or agree with what the other person is saying.

'Sin ninguna duda' – no doubt about it

'Nunca jamás' – never again
'Tienes razón' – you are right
'Te lo juro' – I swear to you
'Ni hablar' – no way
'Ni loco' – no way
'Ni broma' – you must be joking
'¡Segurísimo!' – very sure
'No me digas' – you don't say
'Hombre claro' – of course
'Está claro' – it's clear
'Tiene claro' – it's clear

42. Dealing with situations

Speaking on the telephone

This section is for people who wish to know the telephone customs in Spain, as I must confess I do not know the etiquette in South America.

To an English speaker, telephone exchanges seem very blunt, but this is a perfectly normal way to speak in Spain.

There, you do not answer with 'hola' rather you say 'dígame' (speak to me), 'diga' (speak) or 'dime' (tell me).

When telling someone who you are you say 'soy....' (rather than the third person, as it would be in English) and when asking who they are use '¿quién eres?'

When wishing to be especially polite (for example, when speaking to a client) use the usted form.

For example:

(Telephone rings)

Answering, Pablo: '¿Dígame?'

Maria: 'Soy Maria ¿Eres Pablo?'

Pablo: 'Si, soy Pablo.'

When saying goodbye use 'hasta luego', 'adiós' and so on.

Other useful expressions

'Sonar el teléfono' – the phone rings.

'Responder a la llamada' – answer the call.

Doing something accidentally or on purpose

If you accidentally sat on your friend's glasses you would say, 'lo siento, ha pasado sin querer' (I'm sorry, it happened accidentally). 'Sin querer' (literally, 'without wanting to') is the most common way to express an accident.

Another way to say this is 'no lo he hecho a propósito' (I haven't done it on purpose). You may say it happened 'sin pensar' (without thinking) or 'por distracción' (because you were distracted).

If you're feeling terribly guilty you could also say 'ha sido por mi culpa' (I am to blame) or by way of an apology 'no me he dado cuenta' (I didn't realise).

If something happens by chance (rather than by accident) then it is 'por casualidad'. For example:

'¿Alguien aquí ha dejado un reloj en el vestuario por casualidad?' – has anyone here left a watch in the changing room by accident?

Equally, if you meet someone for the first time who has a lot in common with you, you say '¡Qué casualidad!'

If someone does something on purpose then you could say that they did it 'queriendo,' 'a propósito' or 'adrede'. For example:

'Juan hizo eso adrede para molestarte' – Juan did that on purpose to annoy you.

Reassuring

For the person sat on your glasses, you can reassure them by saying:

'No ha sido culpa tuya' – it wasn't your fault.

'No te preocupes' – don't worry.

'No pasa nada' – don't worry.

To manage to do something

'To manage' as in 'to achieve' something is 'conseguir' or 'lograr' + infinitive. For example:

'Conseguimos conectar a Internet' – we managed to connect to the Internet.

'¿Has logrado hacer los deberes?' – have you managed to do your homework?

'¡Lo conseguí!' – I did it!

Commands

Commands are made with the imperative tense but there are two other commonly used ways I will discuss below.

1) A + infinitive

This is used when you need to get a group of people to do something. For example, if a teacher enters a classroom of rowdy kids they might say 'a callar todos' (everyone be quiet) or when the dinner lady rings the bell for lunch she would say '¡A comer!'

2) Que+ subjunctive

This is used when repeating commands that other people have given. For example, if a child is waiting in the hallway the teacher may send another child to fetch them.

Child A would say to Child B, 'la maestra dice que entres.'

Child A uses the subjunctive because she doesn't know (not being able to read minds)

Making a mistake

If you dial the wrong number you say to the person on the other end 'me he equivocado' from the verb 'equivocarse' (to make a mistake), which you use for everyday errors. If you make a large, potentially life changing mistake use the phrase 'cometer un error'. For data or dates you can also use 'ser erróneo/a' which also mean 'wrong.'

'To mess up' as in 'to get confused,' is the verb 'liarse con.' For example: 'Siempre se lía con las conjugaciones' – she always messes up with the conjugations.

On the subject of language, if you can't think of a word or you say a sentence badly you say 'no me sale la palabra' (literally 'the word doesn't come out of me').

To tell someone off

If you need to discipline someone the verb is 'castigar' (to punish). Likewise if someone is in the dog house for something the phrase is 'está castigado.'

If you need to tell someone off without disciplinary action then the verb is 'reñir.' For example:

'La anciana riñó a los chicos por hacer demasido ruido' – the old lady told the boys off for making too much noise.

If you suddenly start shouting at someone for something that they have done then the term is 'echar una bronca'. For example:

'Mi madre me echó una bronca por no lavar los platos' – my mother told me off for not washing the dishes.

To stand up for yourself is 'plantar cara' while to face a situation is 'enfrentar a algo' (to face something.)

Altercations and dangerous situations

We all run into trouble sometimes and it's important to have some vocabulary to take care of the situation.

If someone lays a hand on you, you say, 'suéltame' (let go of me) or 'déjame en paz' (leave me alone). If they still don't get the message you say '¡Basta ya!' (that's enough!) or '¡Socorro!' (Help!).

If someone is blocking your way you could also say 'apártate' which means 'get out of the way.' It is commonly used and not considered rude.

A general word for 'take care' is 'ten cuidado' ('ten' being the imperative of 'tener'). If someone is about to get run over, however, then you shout, '¡Ojo!' or '¡Cuidado!' (Watch out!)

If something is 'at risk' or 'runs a risk of' use the phrase **corren el riesgo de + infinitive.** If something or someone is in danger then the phrase is **corren peligro de + infinitive**. For example:

'Muchos animales salvajes corren peligro en esta época' – many wild animals are in danger at this time.

If you're recounting a story you may say that you got out of a situation 'por los pelos' (by the skin of our teeth).

If you've been lost at sea for a week and another vessel comes to the rescue you would say '¡Estamos salvados!' (we are saved!).

Something happening suddenly

You have several options for 'to be just about to.' These are, **estar a punto de** or **estar por + infinitive.** For example:

'Estaba a punto de llamarte' – I was just about to call you.

'La carrera está por empezar' – the race is about to start.

'Estar por,' however, means more to have an inclination to do something. For example:

'Estoy por dormir' – I am about to sleep because I feel like sleeping.

'Estamos por tomar un café' – we are about to have a coffee because we like it.

'As soon as' is expressed with **en cuanto + subjunctive** (for present and future) and + indicative (for past and routines). For example:

'En cuanto llegue te llamo' – as soon as he arrives, I'll call you.

'En cuanto comió la cena se durmió' – as soon as he ate dinner he fell asleep.

Another option is **al + infinitive,** which means 'as soon as' or 'upon.' For example:

'Al terminar el trabajo me ducho y me voy – upon finishing work, I take a shower and go.'

Finally, **nada más + infinitive** means 'no sooner than.'
For example:

'Nada más terminar salimos al cine' – no sooner than he had finished, we went to the cinema/no sooner than finishing we went to the cinema.

Noticing things and paying attention

Spanish lacks a definitive verb to say 'to notice.' The closest equivalent is 'darse cuenta,' meaning 'to realise.' For example:

'No me he dado cuenta de que el escalón estaba allí' – I didn't realise that the step was there.

If you want to say 'to notice' as in 'to become aware of' use the verb 'fijarse' (literally, 'to fix yourself on something'). For example:

'El piano es Yamaha, fíjate en la marca' – the piano is Yamaha, notice the brand.

'Notar' means 'to tell' and 'centrarse en algo' –'to concentrate or focus on something.'For example:

'Noto que has estudiado mucho, te centras en el problema' – I can tell that you have studied a lot, you focus on the problem.

Finally, 'to pay attention' in Spanish is either 'prestar atención' (literally, 'to lend attention') or 'hacer caso' (make case). For example:

'Mi hijo no hace caso en clase' – my son doesn't pay attention in class.

Note: The phrase 'tomar nota' means 'to take down an order' or 'to take notes'. It does not mean 'to take notice.'

Driving and car problems

Car vocabulary may not be on the top of the list of things you want to learn but if you breakdown you'll quickly find you really need it, which is why I have written this section. 'To start a car' is 'arrancar el coche' (literally 'to pull out the car'). Most of the other vocabulary is self-explanatory.

Cars

'Avería' – breakdown.

'Averiarse' – to breakdown.
'Abollar' –to dent.
'Una abolladura' – a dent.
'Grúa' – tow truck.
'El capó' – bonnet.
'Maletero' – boot.
'Arañazo' – scratch.
'Remolcar, llevar a remolque' – to tow.
'Tener un pinchazo' – to have a puncher.
'Volante' – steering wheel.

The law
'Una multa' – a fine.
'Poner una multa/ multar' – to fine.
'Sacarse el carnet de conducir' – To get your driver's licence.
'No superar la velocidad' – don't go over the speed limit.
'Reducir la velocidad' –slow down.

Maneuvers
'Atropellarse' – to run over.
'Resultar atropellado' – to get run over.
'Chocar contra/estrellarse' –to bump into.
'Echar gasolina' – get petrol.
'Marchar hacia atrás' – to reverse.
'Poner en punto muerto' –to put into neutral.
'Saltarse el semáforo' – to jump the lights.
'Quedarse sin gasolina' – to run out of petrol.

Technology problems

Some technology differences are: 'to save a file' is 'archivar un documento' while a website is a 'página web' and a system crash is 'bloquearse.' For example: 'Mi móvil se ha bloqueado' – my mobile has crashed.
The rest is pretty straightforward.

The Internet

'Buscador' – search engine.

'Cargar/subir' – to upload.

'Descargar' – to download.

'Foro' – forum.

Software

'Archivo' – file.

'Bloquearse, fallar' – to crash.

'Hacer una copia' – to backup a file.

Hardware

'Altavoz' – speaker.

'Auriculares'– headphones.

'Cargar' – to charge.

'Enchufar/desenchufar' – to plug in/unplug.

'Enchufe' – plug.

'Pantalla' – screen.

'Portátil' – laptop.

'Teclado' – keyboard.

Crime

There aren't as many words for crimes in Spanish as there are in English. Both 'to steal' and 'to rob' are 'robar' and this verb is used for 'to burgle', 'to mug' 'to shoplift' and so on. If someone commits a small crime, such as not paying someone, you will hear people say that they are going to 'poner una denuncia' which means 'to take to court.' If someone is charged with a serious crime then the verb is 'imputar.' For example:

'El juez imputeó a la infanta por crímenes contra la gente' – the judge charged the king's daughter with crimes against the people.'

You may also hear the phrase 'salirse con la suya' which means 'to get away with something minor' or 'to get your own way.' 'Salir impune' meanwhile means to get away with a more serious crime. For example:

'Debería haber pagado la cuenta pero se salió con la suya' – he should have paid the bill but he got away with it.

Crimes

'Asesinar' – to murder.
'Robar' – to rob/steal.
'Secuestrar/raptar' – to kidnap.
'Un carterista' – a pickpocket.

Judicial system

'Crimen' – crime.
'Delito' – criminal.
'Detener' – to arrest.
'Imputar' –to be charged with a crime.
'Pillar/ atrapar' – to catch a criminal.
'Salir impune al cometer un crimen' – to get away with a crime.
'Juez' – judge.
'El jurado' – jury.
'Testigo' – witness.

43. Work and business

Spanish allows several options for the question, 'what do you do?' These are:
- ¿De qué trabajas?
- ¿Qué trabajo haces?
- ¿A qué te dedicas?

'To get a job' is 'conseguir trabajo' while 'to be in charge of something' is 'encargarse de algo' (or literally, 'to charge yourself with something'). For example:

'Me encargo de la caja' – I am in charge of the till.

'¿De qué te encargas?' – what are you in charge of?

To be working on something is 'estoy en ello' for example, 'Estoy en ello ahora mismo' – I am working on it right now. To keep on top of something/someone is 'estar encima de ello/ella.'

Hiring and firing

'Autónomo' – self-employed.

'Contractar a alguien' – to hire.

'Despedir a alguien' – to fire.

'Dimitir' –to resign.

'Emplear' – to employ.

'Empleado' – employed.

'Desempleado' – unemployed.

'Ser despedido por reducción de plantilla' – to be made redundant.

'Plantilla' – staff.

Timetables

'Turno' – shift.

'Tiempo parcial' – full time.

'Tiempo completo' – part time.

'Tener un día libre' – to take the day off.
'Dar la baja por enfermedad' – take a day off sick.

Training
'Becario' – intern.
'Formarse' – to train professionally.
'La formación' – training.
'Hacer prácticas' – to do an internship.
'Perfil' – (profile) background.
'Requisito' – requirement.
'Título' – qualification.

Business
'To set up a business' is 'montar un negocio' while 'to run a company' is 'dirigir una empresa'

Useful business words
'Cifras' – figures.
'Contraoferta' – to counter offer.
'Emprendedor' – entrepreneur.
'Invertir' – to invest.
'Inversión' – investment.
'Pérdida' – loss.
'Poner impuestos' – to tax.
'Renta' – profit.
'Rentable' – profitable.
'Tramitar' – to carry out a transaction.
'Trato hecho' – done deal.

44. Education and ability

To be good or bad at something

In Spanish there are several ways to say that you are good or bad at something. The most common being :

Ser bueno/malo en + noun or **ser bueno/malo + gerund**

For example:

'Soy bueno en natación pero soy malo corriendo' – I am good at swimming but I am bad at running.

Another way to say this is **se le da bien/mal + noun or infinitive**

For example:

'Se le da bien jugar a fútbol' – he is good at playing football.

To be capable at something is **soy capaz + de + infinitive**.

For example:

'Soy capaz de hacer el trabajo y ella es capaz de organizar la reunión– I am capable of doing the work and she is capable of organising the meeting.

As in English there are many more ways to say that you're not good at something or find it difficult. Here are some phrases.

'Ser negada para algo' – to be hopeless/useless at something.
'Le resulta difícil/fácil algo' – to find something difficult or easy.
'Le cuesta algo' – to find something difficult (literally, something costs you.)
'Ser torpe + gerund' – to be very bad at something (literally, to be clumsy at something.)
'Ser un desastre + gerund' – to be a disaster at something.
'No estoy llegando a ninguna parte' – I am not getting anywhere.

Education

To be stuck on a problem is 'bloquearse con,' while 'bastarle con' means to scrape by. For example:

'Estamos bloqueados con la operación del martes' – we are stuck on the maths problem.

'Me basta con pasar el examen con una nota mínima' – I scraped by with a minimum mark.

More useful words
Exams

'To pass' is 'aprobar' while 'to fail' is 'suspender.'

'Corregir' – to mark.

'Copiar' – to cheat in an exam (while 'un copión' means a cheat in exams).

'Presentarse al examen' – to take an exam.

'Recuperar el examen' – to retake an exam.

'Sacar notas' – to get marks.

'Temario' – syllabus.

'Trimestre' – term.

Enrolling in a course

'Matricularse' – to enrol.

'Matrícula' – enrolment.

'Solicitar' – to apply for.

'Solicitud' – application.

'Tazas' – fees.

Subjects and qualifications

'Carrera' – degree.

'Asignaturas, materia' – subjects.

45. Verb families

When prefix is added onto a verb to create a new meaning this is called a compound verb (verbo compuesto). Spanish has over 100 of these and they are very useful as the new verb will continue to be conjugated and pronounced in exactly the same way as the original (but with an 'add on' at the beginning). For example 'mantener' (to maintain/keep) comes from the 'tener' verb family meaning that in present it is 'mantengo', 'mantiene', in preterite 'mantuve' and 'mantuvo' and in imperfect 'mantenía' and so on.

Cargar
Sobrecargar – to overload.
Cargado – Loaded.

Cubrir
Recubrir – to paint over.

Decir
Bendecir – to bless.
Contradecir – to contradict.
Desdecir – to deny.
Maldecir – to curse.
Predecir – to predict.

Escribir
Describir – to describe.
Inscribir – to inscribe.
Prescribir – to prohibit (false friend).
Subscribir – to subscribe.
Transcribir – to transcribe.

Sobrescribir – to overwrite.

Hacer
Contrahacer - to counterfit/ to forge.
Deshacer – to undo/ to unpack/ to cancel.
Quehacer – chores (a noun).
Rehacer – To redo.

Meter
Cometer – to commit a crime.
Prometer – to promise.
Comprometer – to commit (comprometerse – to get engaged).
Someter – to submit (to dominate) e.g 'Me someto a la prueba' – submit to the trial.

Meter changes depending on the preposition
Meterse en – or to interfere/or to get into something (e.g. music).
Meterse a hacer algo – to take up something (e.g. tennis).
Meterse con alguien – to pick on/ to tease someone.

Pagar
Prepagar – to prepay (But pagar por delante is better).
Propagar – to disseminate/ to spread.
Repagar – to repay or pay too much.
Apagar – to turn off/ extinguish.

Parar
Reparar – to repair.
Preparar – to prepare.
Separar – to separate.
Disparar – to shoot.

Comparar – to compare.

Poner

Componer – To compose.

Contraponer – To constrast (contrapuesto – noun) or oppose.

Disponer – To be available.

Exponer – To expose/ exibit/ show.

Imponer – To impose.

Oponer – To oppose.

Posponer – To postpone.

Proponer – To propose.

Reponer – To replace.

Suponer – To suppose.

Yuxtaponer – To juxtapose.

Preciar

Apreciar – to appreciate/ to grow in value.

Depreciar – to depreciate.

Despreciar – to despise/ to have no regard.

Seguir

Perseguir – to chaise.

Conseguir – to achieve/ to manage to/ to get.

Sentir

Asentir – to assent (agree)/ to nod.

Consentir – to consent/ agree.

Disentir – to dissent/ disagree.

Presentir – to foresee.

Resentir – to suffer/ to be weakened.

Tener

Abstener – to abstain.

Mantener – to maintain.

Atenerse – to obey.

Contener – to contain.

Detener – to detain.

Entretener – to entertain.

Obtener – to obtain.

Retener – to retain/ hold back/ deduct.

Sostener – to sustain.

Traer

Abstraer – to abstract.

Atraer – to attract.

Contraer – to contract.

Distraer – to distract.

Extraer – to extract/ to take out – e.g. Tooth.

Retraer – retract.

Substraer – to subtract/ steal/ take away.

Venir

Avenir – to reconcile/ come to an agreement.

Contravenir – to infringe/ violate/ contravene.

Convenir – to be suitable.

Intervenir – to intervene.

Prevenir – to prevent/ warn.

Sobrevenir – to happen suddenly.

Provenir – to come from.

Ver

Prever – to foresee ('sin noticias previas' – without notice).

Entrever – to glimpse.

Vivir
Bienvivir – to live well/ comfortably.
Malvivir – to live badly.
Convivir – to coexist/live with.
Desvivirse – to devote yourself.
Revivir – to revive.
Sobrevivir – to survive.

Querer
Adquirer – To acquire.
Requirir – to require.

46. What's the verb?

Finding your phrasal verbs in Spanish

Phrasal verbs are a verb + preposition –for example, 'take up', 'give up', 'go out with someone' and so on. They are everywhere in English meaning that half the time you are searching for a verb it is a phrasal. They don't exist in Spanish, but the more formal equivalent does, meaning that when trying to express a phrasal verb think of its formal version in English. Normally you'll find this is the verb in Spanish. For example:

'I don't know how she <u>puts up with</u> him' is 'no sé como le <u>tolera</u>.'

Phrasal verb equivalents

To be locked in – quedarse encerrado/a.

To be locked out – quedarse afuera (sin llaves).

To bring down/shoot down – derribar.

To blow up (a building) – explotar.

To blow up a balloon – inflar

To build up – acumular.

To catch up with work – ponerse al día.

To catch up with someone (physically) – alcanzar.

To check out – pagar y marcharse.

To come out (publish) – publicar. *'La revista se publica mensualmente' – The magazine comes out monthly.*

To come down to – reducirse. *'El debate se redujo a si era necesaria una reforma de la educación' – the debate came down to whether education reform was needed.*

To cut down on – reducir.

To draw attention to – llamar la atención.

To draw up a plan – elaborar un plan.

To end up – acabar + gerund.

To face up to something – Enfrentar a algo.

To fall behind – quedarse atrás/ retrasarse.

To get around (idea) – difundirse. *'El rumor se difundio rápidamente'* – *The rumour got around quickly.*

To get something across – transmitir.

To get away with – salir impune/salir con la suya.

To get something back – recuperar.

To get by in a language – defenderse.

To get going – pongamos en marcha.

To get on well – llevarse bien.

To get on/in – subir.

To get off/out – bajar.

To get to the point – ir al grano.

To get through to – establecer contacto.

To get together as a couple – emparejarse.

To get up – levantarse.

To go off (electricity cut) – saltar la luz.

To go over (rehearse) – ensayar. *'Ensayémoslo una vez mas'* – *Let's go over it one more time.*

To go out (light) – irse la luz.

To go up to – acercarse.

To go out with someone – salir con alguien.

To lean against – apoyarse en.

To light up (joy) – iluminarse. *'Se le iluminó la cara'* – *his face lit up.*

To listen up – escuchar bien.

To look forward to – esperar con ilusión.

To make out (understand) – captar. *'No puedo captar lo que dicen'* – *I can't make out what they are saying.'*

To overpower someone – reducir. *'La policía redujo al hombre que amenazaba con tirarse del puente* – *The police overpowered a man who threatened to jump from a bridge.*

To pass out – quedarse sin sentido.

To pick up – recoger.

To put up with – tolerar.

To set off – activar.

To show up – presentarse. *'El profesor no se presentó a la clase' – The teacher didn't show up for class.*

To slow down – reducir la velocidad.

To stay in touch – seguir en contacto.

To stand in the way of – impedir.

To stand up to someone – plantar cara a alguien.

To stay up late – quedarse hasta tarde.

To take back an insult – retirar.

To take in (welcome) – acoger. *'El gobierno acogió a los refugiados' – the government took in the refugees.*

To take up (an offer) – aceptar.

To tear up – romper. *'No rompas esa foto' – don't tear up that photo.*

To tear off/out – arrancar.

'No puedo arrancar esta página. ¿Me la arrancas?' – I can't tear off/out the page. Can you tear it off for me?

To turn down a job – rechazar un puesto.

To turn back – dar media vuelta.

To turn out – resultar. *'Resulta que todo el mundo lo sabía menos yo' – it turns out everyone knew except me.*

To use up – consumar. *'No consumas toda la batería hoy' – don't use up all the battery today.*

To wake up – despertarse.

47. Collocations

Collocations are verb + noun or adjective combinations that make an expression. I have divided the collocations here by verb rather than vocabulary set to make them easier to memorise.

Tener
Tener lugar – to take place.
Tener en cuenta – to take into account.
Tener sentido – to make sense.
Tener miedo – to be scared.
Tener prisa – to be in a hurry.
Tener calor/frío – to be hot/cold (a person).

Dar
Dar cuerda – to wind up.
Darse cuenta – to realise something.
Dar la hora - to strike the hour/ tell the time.
Dar miedo – to scare.
Dar la cara – to confront a situation.
Dar largas – to delay a reply.
Dar calabazas – to reject someone romantically.
Dar por vencido – to give up.
Dar por terminado – to be sure it's finished.
Dar por sentado – to take for granted, to assume.
Echar un vistazo – to take a look.
Dar una mano – to lend a hand.

Pasar
Pasar por – to pass by somewhere.

Pasarse – to go too far with an issue.
Pasar buen/ mal rato – to have a good time.
Pasar por alto – to overlook.

Hacer
Hacer una visita – to pay a visit.
Hacer un viaje – to go on a trip.
Hacer caso – to pay attention.
Hacer frío/calor – to be cold/hot (the weather).
Hacer turnos – to take turns.
Hacer progreso – to make progress.
Hacer una pregunta – to ask a question.

More collocations
Convocar un reunión – to call a meeting.
Dirigir una empresa – to run a company.
Estar a dieta – to go on a diet.
Pedir una cita – to make an appointment
Poner un ejemplo – to give an example
Hacer una huelga – to go on strike.
Presentarse al examen – to take an exam.
Sacar un tema – to bring up a subject.
Proyectar una película – to show a film.

48. Writing

Note that in writing the date, the day number is followed by de, which again follows the name of the month. The convention is to write dates: day–month–year. More informally you can write this information in numerals: 11–10–02. For example: 11 de octubre de 2002.

Greetings

In formal letters when you do not know the person to whom you are writing:
Muy señor mío/ muy señora mía/ muy señores míos:
The Spanish equivalent of 'to whom it may concern is 'a quién corresponda'.
A less formal option is the greeting using the word estimado/da:
Estimado señor: Estimada señora: Estimados señores:
This opening appears on the left–hand side. <u>Note the use of the colon.</u>

In informal letters or when you know the address well, an opening following querido/da is appropriate:
Querido Rafael/Querida Beatriz/Queridos Beatriz y Rafael/Querido Papá:

Ending the letter

Modern practice, particularly in Spain, is to keep endings short. The following should be adequate for most situations. Your signature should follow directly below, as it would in English.

Formal endings

A la espera de sus prontas noticias, le saluda atentamente.
Le saluda atentamente.
Atentamente.

Less formal endings

Un cordial saludo.
Cordialmente.

In friendly personal letters, the following are often used:
Un abrazo/un fuerte abrazo/un fuerte abrazo de tu amigo,
The ending 'un abrazo' is often used in business correspondence and even in internal company memos or emails, where a friendly relationship exists between the parties.
Typical endings for friends and family are:
Un afectuoso [or cariñoso] saludo,
Afectuosamente, Un beso, Besos, Con todo mi cariño.

Additional information

And finally...

Thank you for reading this book, I hope you found it useful. If you have a moment please leave a review on the site where you bought it or on Good Reads. It is much appreciated. Happy learning! AJ.

Thinking about teaching TEFL English?

Then check out The Ultimate English as a Second Language Teaching Manual and discover a skill that will serve you for the rest of your life.

The Ultimate ESL Teaching Manual is a 395 page book containing lesson plans, drills and speaking activities for every grammar point – yes, every grammar point even the ones that go way beyond what you would find at an average academy. It also contains methodology, games, vocabulary sets and a whole host of other stuff to make your classes special.

Available now in ebook and paperback at Amazon. Just type B01FFRNGGC into the search bar and you'll find it.

Or for more information visit our website www.bilinguanation.com

Some of our reviews on Amazon

Great for time-strapped English teachers, by Amazon Customer

This is a one-stop shop for preparing powerful classes that throws out the need for costly and confusing text books. Andromeda Jones has poured a wealth of knowledge and experience into this book. It's saving me a lot of time in preparations and research. ★★★★★

A top read, by Sheila Longden

What a great book! Andromeda's knowledge and experience shines through. She gets straight to the point, gives very clear grammar explanations and loads of practical help. I'm already using it very successfully with my students and have recommended it to other teachers. Thank you. ★★★★★

Good book, saved me hours of prep, by TeacherA24

Well laid out, each grammar point comes with its own speaking activities and there are hundreds of vocabulary sets at the back so you won't run out of ideas about what to teach your students. ★★★★★

Printed in Great Britain
by Amazon